The Thread of Mu'awiya

The Thread of Mu'awiya

The Making of a Marja' Taqlid

Linda S. Walbridge

Edited by
John Walbridge

The Ramsay Press

Published by

The Ramsay Press

Bloomington, Indiana

ISBN: 0615957560
ISBN-13: 9780615957562

To the memory of
Abdul Majid Al-Khoei,
who died
to bring reconciliation
to his country,

and to Linda's friend and collaborator,
Talib Aziz

إن بيني وبين النّاس شعرة
إذا أرخوا شددت وإذا شدّوا أرخيت

I have a thread connecting me to every man.
When he loosens it, I tighten it,
and when he tightens it, I loosen it.

The Caliph Muʿawiya

CONTENTS

Foreword

John Walbridge

BEFORE HER UNTIMELY DEATH from breast cancer in 2002 at the age of 56, my wife Linda Strickland Walbridge was planning to resume a study of networks of Arab Shi'ite leadership that she had begun in the early 1990s. The present work is an early draft that she completed in about 1996 but had not been satisfied with. Since she did not live to revise the work as she would have wished but since the manuscript is essentially complete, contains a great deal of valuable information, and has proven useful to several other scholars working in related areas, I have taken it upon myself to edit it for publication. I hope that it will preserve her distinctive street anthropologist voice and will serve as a memorial to her and to her passion for the peoples of the Islamic world.

IN 1987 LINDA APPLIED for the Ph.D. program in anthropology at Wayne State University in Detroit. Her reasons for choosing Wayne State were practical: it was affordable, and she could do her dissertation research on the Arab community of Dearborn. It was a good choice. She quickly made friends in the Arab community, which at that time was largely Lebanese Shi'ite. Her Baha'i background gave her an understanding of Shi'ite history, and her pious Catholic childhood was a surprisingly good basis for understanding the sorrowful fervor of Shi'ite spirituality. Finally, her background in psychology helped her understand factors like family dynamics. She also quickly made friends among the ulama, who liked her because she understood what they were going through but was not part of their community, so that they could relax around her and ask her advice about dealing with their rather trying parishioners. The result of her Ph.D. work was her dissertation on the religious life of Dearborn, later published as *Without Forgetting the Imam: Lebanese Shi'ism in an American Community* (Detroit: Wayne State University Press, 1997). Shortly after she finished her thesis in 1991, we moved to Columbia University, where she became the assistant director of the Middle East Institute. In 1993 I was offered a job at Indiana University, and Linda moved there soon after.

Without a regular position at Indiana University, Linda returned to her research, publishing her dissertation and picking up her research on Shi'ism where she had left off. This time she turned seriously to the question of religious leadership and, in particular, the question of how a marja' taqlid, a grand ayatollah, establishes himself and spreads his influence. By this time she had a considerable circle of friends among Arab Shi'ite ulama in the West. In the mid-1990s she traveled to various Shi'ite communities in America and Britain, interviewing their leaders and trying to understand how they interacted with each other and with the clerical establishments in their home countries, particularly Iraq. It was at this time that she repeatedly heard the saying that forms the title of this book. The Caliph Mu'awiya, a villain in Shi'ite history for his opposition to the Imam 'Ali but respected as a master politician, is said to have said, "I have a thread connecting me to every man. When he loosens it, I tighten it, and when he tightens it, I loosen it." The point was that even ulama who bitterly opposed each other still kept connections with their rivals.

In 1995 she wrote an article, partly based on the present book, arguing that the center of gravity of world Shi'ism had shifted from Iran to Iraq, since the Iranian religious leadership had discredited itself due to its involvement in politics, and the key figure was now Ayatollah Sistani, the generally recognized successor to Ayatollah al-Khu'i. Her attempts to publish the article were unsuccessful, for reviewers, all experts on Iranian Shi'ism, pointed out that it was preposterous to think that the influence of the persecuted ulama of Najaf and Karbala could possibly be compared to the established theocracy of Iran. After several rejections, Linda concluded that if she was having this kind of trouble, then others were too, so she solicited articles for an edited volume on alternative forms of Shi'ite leadership. This was published as *The Most Learned of the Shi'a: The Institution of the Marja' Taqlid* (New York: Oxford University Press, 2001). Her article was "The Counterreformation: Becoming a *Marja'* in the Modern World." The relevance of the article has since been more generally appreciated.

Linda wrote the present book in the summer of 1996. She was not satisfied with it and set it aside, planning to revise it on the basis of further research. At that point events intervened. The academic year 1996–97 was extraordinarily turbulent in our family, culminating in the spring with Linda's discovery that she had breast cancer. We had also both received Fulbrights: Linda to Indonesia and I to Pakistan. She began to return to her Shi'ite research in the winter and spring of 1998 when she joined me in Pakistan and began making contacts among the Pakistani Shi'a. These contacts are not reflected in this book, but she had drafted an article on one of her friends that I finished and published as "Master Singer of Pakistan: Baba Shafqat," in Frances Trix, John Walbridge, and Linda S. Walbridge, *Muslim Voices in the Modern World* (New York: Palgrave Macmillan, 2008).

Once again events intervened. At the beginning of May 1998, John Joseph, the Catholic bishop of Feisalabad in Pakistan, commited suicide in front of a courthouse in protest against the blasphemy laws that were being used to persecute local Christians. Since it took place during the Shi'ite mourning period of 'Ashura, Linda thought that it might involve Shi'ite symbolism (apparently it did not), but it was clearly a pivotal event in the history of Pakistani Christianity, and there was obviously no other trained observer in the country with background in both religious minorities in the Islamic world and Catholicism. Linda threw herself into this project, the sort of research opportunity that comes once in a lifetime, if it comes at all. She conducted extensive interviews all over the country, beginning a few days after the bishop's death. This project occupied her through 2001, including follow-up visits to Pakistan in 1999 and 2000–1. The result was her best book, *The Christians of Pakistan: The Passion of Bishop John Joseph* (London, New York: Routledge/Curzon, 2002).

With her work on the Pakistani Christians completed and the resultant book and a reader for anthropology classes in press, she planned to return to her work on Shi'ism, but her breast cancer had recurred. Shortly before her death she learned that she had been awarded a two-year fellowship from the Russell-Sage Foundation to complete this project, but by then the cancer had reached her brain, and on 9 December 2002 she passed away. Her tombstone is inscribed with a cross embraced by a crescent moon and reads:

LINDA STRICKLAND WALBRIDGE
ANTHROPOLOGIST, AUTHOR,
ADVENTURER, FRIEND

THE PRESENT BOOK is not what Linda wished to have published and should therefore be used with some reserve. Almost twenty years have passed, and many things have happened in the Shi'a world, notably the fall of Saddam Hussein and the resurgence of Shi'ism in Iraq. It does not even include the results of her research after July 1996, though as I have said, in the last six years of her life, she mostly worked on other things. Her manuscript did not contain notes, though I have tried to supply references for quotations from published sources. She had not prepared a bibliography. I have supplied one from her article in *The Most Learned of the Shi'a* with a few additions. Mostly, she wrote from the interviews she had conducted herself. These interviews have been deposited with her papers in the archives of Notre Dame University in South Bend, Indiana. This collection also includes her field notes and other materials for her work on the Lebanese Shi'a in Dearborn and the Pakistani Christians, in addition to her personal papers. These materials are not restricted, but interested researchers should contact the Notre Dame Archives to see whether they have been processed and are accessible.

I am presenting the manuscript largely as Linda left it. I have not tried to update the content. Where Linda indicated that there should be a footnote, I have tried to supply the reference. Where I have not been able to find her source, I have indicated that fact. In a few places her collaborator Talib Aziz has supplied corrections and references. I have copyedited the manuscript: correcting spelling, standardizing format, and the like. Except in cases where there are well-established English forms ("Tehran"), I have standardized the spelling of Arabic and Persian words and names, using the normal scholarly transliteration without diacritics. Since most of the individuals, places, and words are Arabic, I have used Arabic transliteration for Persian names. The system will be clear enough for specialists.

Something also needs to be said about the role of her friend Talib Aziz. Linda had hoped to have Talib, an expert on contemporary Arab Shi'ite thought, as a co-author in the final book, and he was clearly an important source of information for her in the present version. I asked him if he wished to assume this role, but he declined, preferring that the book remain as Linda left it as a memorial to his friend. She would certainly have wished to acknowledge his role, which I am pleased to do, but the opinions expressed are Linda's, not Talib's.

I cannot make the acknowledgements that Linda would have, since I cannot now reconstruct her intellectual obligations or know who would have wanted to remain anonymous. She would have wished me to thank all those she interviewed for this book, whether named in the book or not. She would have particularly wished to thank the ulama who received her with such hospitality and answered her questions with frankness. However, I can especially mention the Qazwini family—Hassan, Mustafa, and their father Murtada—who were very generous with their time and knowledge. Laith Kubba and his wife Jane, Nadeem Kazmi, and his uncle Baba Shafqat were all dear to Linda and gave her friendship, support, information, understanding, and hospitality. The Al-Khoei Foundation in London and particularly Yousif and Abdul Majid Al-Khoei were central to her work and to her conception of the institution of the marja'iya. It is to Majid, whose tragic death came too soon after Linda's, and to Talib Aziz, her friend, collaborator, and informant that I dedicate this book.

Since this book represents something of a memorial to Linda, I will close my introduction with the eulogy that I delivered at her funeral.

A EULOGY FOR LINDA WALBRIDGE

Delivered by her husband

IN AN OLD ISLAMIC BOOK IT IS WRITTEN: "Jesus the Messiah said, 'This world is a bridge. Cross it but do not linger.'"

When I wondered who might deliver Linda's eulogy, I realized that others knew only fragments of her life: Linda the friend, Linda the scholar, Linda the adventuress, Linda Walbridge, that impossible woman. Only I knew something of the whole.

Linda will be remembered for her writings about the people of the East, but the burning desire of her childhood was to go to the American West. She was restless in her safe suburban upbringing and sensed vaguely that she needed to search for something she would not find there. And so at age nineteen she joined VISTA, the domestic equivalent of the Peace Corps, and went off to the Southwest. There, as I later teased her, she pestered the Navajo. The Navajo seem to have taken this in good spirit, and Linda certainly learned enough from them to justify her stay in New Mexico. Having survived a car crash that might have killed her, she returned to put herself through college in Connecticut.

It is at this point that her quest became spiritual. Linda had grown up a good Catholic girl, the daughter and granddaughter of iron-willed English Catholic women. As a little girl she had loved the ritual life of the pre-Vatican II church: the morning Mass in Latin, the statues of the Blessed Virgin and the saints, and the comfortable certainties of those days. But even as a little girl she had wondered about the people who were not part of that safe world, the strange heathen peoples whom the missionaries met. When she went west, she first saw the flaws of the Church, that greatest of human institutions, and she saw them with the uncompromising eyes of the young.

She came back from New Mexico a Baha'i and remained a Baha'i for thirty years. She saw in the Baha'i Faith the universality that she missed in Catholicism. She loved the openness of the Baha'is to diversity. She remained very much a Catholic Baha'i. She venerated the saints of the Baha'is as she had the saints of her childhood. She became closest to the Iranian and Arab Baha'is, with their heritage of martyrdom and their deep, ultimately Islamic cultural heritage. She threw herself heart and soul into the Baha'i Faith, and served it well and unstintingly for many years.

It is at this point that I enter the picture. I was a new Baha'i myself in 1970 and a student at Yale. With a friend of mine, an astronomy student, I went to a meeting that Linda was running. Linda was going to college across town, but she preferred Yale. "I like smart men," she explained. I vividly remember her that afternoon—in charge, a flash of blond hair, unfashionably elegant eye makeup, and a silky scarlet dress that was short even by the standards of those happy days. She was not interested in me, nor in my astronomer friend. But when I came back to Yale a year later she was engaged to the astronomer—a very smart man. He was, however, gone a lot in the evenings, and so I ended up with the girl, a coup that continues to give me quiet male satisfaction. And thus we were married, a little over thirty years ago.

Soon after that I announced that we should go to Beirut for a year for my studies. She arranged to study for a Master's in psychology while we were there. Her splendid Arabic and English diploma was smuggled out to Cyprus at the height of the civil war. Beirut was the turning point in her life, though she didn't know it yet. She was directly exposed to the rich spiritual tradition of the Middle East and especially to Islam. When it was time to go back to the Middle East a few years later, she readily quit her job, packed the baby, and set off for Iran—though revolution intervened and we ended up in Jordan instead. My mother pleaded as we left, "Promise me, dears, if anything happens, go straight to the American embassy." Even then we knew better.

We returned some months later and settled in Upper Michigan for eight years. It was a difficult time for Linda. She had given up her career for me and, more important, for our children. She never regretted giving those years to our sons, but they were hard years. We were poor, I was away at work every day, and it was winter seven months a year, and summer seven weeks. This was an exhausting and lonely time for Linda. Our children, though, remember it as a happy time, "when Mom baked."

But a year or two into our stay in Upper Michigan, she had the first of the three "true dreams," as the Arabs call them, that were to mark off the periods of the rest of her life. She dreamed that the Caliph Abu Bakr, the first of the Prophet Muhammad's successors, put a cloak around her and said, "You are my daughter." It was the beginning of a period of involvement with Islam and with Arabs. She read everything she could find about the Islamic world and wrote four unpublished novels about it. When I was offered an editing job that could be done anywhere, she decided to go back to graduate school and get her Ph.D. in anthropology. She went to Wayne State University, and we settled in Dearborn, where there is a large immigrant Arab community. She began researching her dissertation on the religious life of the Lebanese Shi'ite community there.

It was at this point that she had her second true dream. She dreamed that she was in a caravan crossing the desert. She looked around, wondering where she was. "I am with the Imam Husayn," she thought and then she awoke. Husayn was the grandson of the Prophet Muhammad. Linda had dreamed that she was with him on his last journey to Karbala, where he and the handful of men with him would face martyrdom at the hands of a tyrant and his womenfolk would be carried off into suffering and exile.

Linda loved the Lebanese Shi'ites. They were independent and cantankerous. Her childhood Catholicism was an unexpected window into their religious life, a life dominated by the memory of the tragedy of Karbala and the guilt of still living in a world unredeemed when their leader and champion had died for the sake of justice. They instinctively knew that they could trust her and told her the most extraordinary things—some of which, she joked, could only be published in the posthumous book that she fortunately never wrote. Stranger still, the Shi'ite clergy she met liked and trusted her. They often consulted her about pastoral problems. She was someone who understood them and their problems, who understood America, but who was not a Muslim herself, so they didn't have to play a role with her. A Shi'ite friend once said, "Linda, you must become a Muslim, but not yet." This period is preserved in her first book, *Without Forgetting the Imam.*

About the time she graduated, we both got jobs at Columbia University in New York. Two years later, in 1993, I was offered a job here at Indiana University. It was the beginning of the most difficult, but also the most productive period of Linda's life. It was, on the one hand, the time of Linda's battles with authority. The first set the pattern, when she was arrested and handcuffed at the George Washington Bridge for driving in a car pool lane without a current insurance card. That resulted in a number of news stories and ended with her ruthless New York lawyer successfully suing the Port Authority of New York and New Jersey. Better known in Bloomington was her hunger strike under President Brand's window when doctored documents were used in my tenure case. The memory of that has now outlived her at Indiana University and will most likely outlive me and any other memory of my career here.

She didn't always win her battles—she lost a bitter fight to keep Nathaniel from being expelled from eighth grade, for example—but once she had taken a stand, she did not back down. She had no patience with pretension, and she saw quite accurately into people's souls. And so people either admired her for her courage and honesty or they feared her because she saw through them. There was not much in between.

It was about then that she had the last of her true dreams: she dreamed that she had breast cancer. She demanded a biopsy, despite the doctor's insistence that the lump she found did not look like cancer. And when it was cancer, she insisted on an immediate mastectomy. Five weeks later she set out for a semester in Indonesia and a few months later joined me in Pakistan.

Pakistan, not me, was the true love of her life. She loved the bustling confusion of the country, the warmth of the people, and the passion with which they pursued their causes, hobbies, and obsessions. She loved the clothes with their bright colors, exuberant decoration, and yards of flowing fabrics. Pakistan, like India, is a land of castes, and Linda had a caste. She was a memsahib, of the adventurous sort. The British used to say of such people that they "loved India," which was not always a compliment.

But the Pakistanis understood her and loved her because she loved them and sometimes followed her with a loyalty and devotion that has no counterpart in our egalitarian society.

It was during this stay that she began the project that is the chief justification of her life, her book on the Christians of Pakistan. She was by this time no longer a Baha'i. That is not a story to tell here. The real cause was that the Baha'i community as it existed in America failed to embody the values of ritual and inner life that were the valuable kernel of her Catholic childhood. Our two young cooks would sometimes take her to mass, proudly picking her up in a rickshaw and taking her to the local church, St. Mary's. Linda loved the fervor and simplicity of the services. Especially she loved the singing of psalms, which had been translated into Punjabi poetry by a Sikh convert a century ago. The Pakistani Christians, for the most part a poor and despised minority, would sing their hearts out, recognizing their own torment in David's pain. They needed Linda, and so she identified with them.

It was one Thursday morning in May of 1998, the anniversary of the martyrdom of the Imam Husayn, of whom Linda had once dreamed. We read in the paper that the Roman Catholic bishop of Faisalabad had shot himself in front of a courthouse in protest at the blasphemy laws. That Sunday we went to church at the Catholic cathedral of Lahore. On the way we passed through the main square of Lahore (known, incongruously, as Charing Cross) and saw a group of Christian men protesting in sackcloth, ashes, and chains. "Stop," Linda yelled to the driver. They were, she found, reacting to the Bishop's death. Then at the cathedral a young priest preached a fiery sermon comparing the Bishop to Christ.

Clearly, something important was happening. She went the next day to the offices of the Archdiocese, where she was received by the Vicar-General. This was Father Mani, among other things the headmaster of the school to which memorial donations are being made in Linda's memory. Linda explained that she was considering writing a book on the Bishop. "Ah," said Father Mani, "we decided last night that we wanted someone to write a book. Let me call and make you some appointments."

Linda spent the next months crisscrossing Pakistan in the ferocious heat of summer, going to difficult and sometimes dangerous places, and meeting extraordinary people. The Christians, she discovered—particularly the ordinary people—desperately wanted their story told to the world. They wanted Linda to tell the story of their bishop, whom they loved and venerated as a martyr and a saint. She went back to Pakistan twice more and wrote the book, weaving together the story of the martyred bishop, the history of this orphaned community of Christians, and the efforts of their leaders to serve and protect them. Her book—*The Christians of Pakistan: the Passion of Bishop John Joseph*—is now published, and Linda received her first copies a few weeks before she died.

Thus the last of her true dreams, the warning of cancer, had won her five years to do what she considered to be the one truly important thing in her professional life, the one thing as important as her children.

When Linda fell ill last winter, she sensed that something was badly wrong and that she might die. She hurried to complete work on *The Christians of Pakistan* and on the anthropology reader that she was doing with her friend April Sievert. There were, after all, deadlines to be met, and she could not very well meet them if she were dead. She was not afraid of dying: she was not really afraid of anything. She still had hope, of course, and had new projects she wanted to do. Three weeks before her death she was awarded a grant to continue her study of Shi'ite clergy in America. She had started another reader and had assigned all the articles at a time when she could barely walk unaided. She would have liked to have done the other things she planned, but she had seen too much of death and insecurity in the Third World, and was far too unsentimental, to be angry at her approaching end.

The prayers we read today speak of the certainty of resurrection. I don't know whether Linda believed that. I don't think she thought very much about which religions and which doctrines were true. But she believed in religion from the depths of her soul. She believed that religion was a fundamental part of being human. She liked religious people, and they knew that she understood them and accepted them. She had seen too many faiths to have kept the one simple faith of her childhood. She had gone up onto the mountain and looked out across the Jordan. There she saw the promised land spread out before her in all the richness and diversity of human religious experience.

Now she has crossed over to whatever it is that awaits us all, leaving her friends, of so many faiths, still lingering on the bridge.

The Thread of Mu'awiya

Chapter One

Ayatollah al-Khu'i and the Marja'iya

SAYYID MAJID AL-KHU'I ASKED HIS MOTHER, "Why, if I work and study, don't I get a salary like everybody else?" His mother agreed to intervene on his behalf with his father, the Grand Ayatollah Abu'l-Qasim al-Khu'i. The next day Ayatollah al-Khu'i said to his son, "You know how to get a salary. You go to the office and take an exam like any other student. If you pass it, you get a salary. Why don't you just go take this exam?" Majid went to the office where the exams were administered and told the ulama (clerics; singular, 'alim) in charge that he wanted to take the exam that would make him officially one of his father's students. "But you don't need to take an exam," one of the ulama responded. "I know," said Majid, "but I want a salary and can't have one unless I have passed the exam." During the exam, Majid became worried and started to have doubts about whether he really needed this salary after all. What if he did not do well and embarrassed his father before the ulama? His fears seem to have been unfounded. His father called him to his presence that night and said, "Very good. I am happy. Now you can have your salary."

However, after several months he said to his father, "Listen, Daddy, you give me the same salary that is normally given to students. But there is a difference between me and the others. First, when I go to make ziyara (visitation) to the holy shrines, the people at the bus expect me to pay. I am the son of the grand ayatollah, so everyone looks to me to pay. But one bus ride and my salary is gone. And it is not fair for me to keep my hand closed and wait for someone else to pay. I don't like that. Second, other students also have salaries from other ulama, but I don't have that. I just have a salary from you. It is not enough." His father replied,

"There is another difference as well. When I give to other students, I give two Iraqi dinars and they have to live on this. But you live at home and your food and clothes are free and your books are free. The two dinars are just your pocket money."

There was about a sixty-five-year difference in age between the Grand Ayatollah and his son. Majid tried to persuade his father that times had changed and that, due to the oil money flowing into Iraq, many people were quite prosperous. But his father insisted that a marja' taqlid (the exemplar, the one whom the Shi'a emulate) must live more humbly than the rest of the people. After all, when a poor peasant came to Najaf to pay the sahm al-Imam (the religious tax) to him as the representative of the Hidden Imam, was it fair for him to have luxuries such as a car, a refrigerator, a television? It was not proper for him to waste the Imam's money on luxuries for himself and his family.

Ayatollah al-Khu'i finally did accept a car as a gift from some wealthy Kuwaiti Shi'ite. The car enabled him to commute the five kilometers from Kufa, where the family lived, to the mosque and his offices in Najaf more efficiently than by the two-horse carriage that he was accustomed to travelling in. However, money always remained an issue. He would, for example, turn off the lights as he left a room so as "not to waste the Imam's money."

When his car needed repair one day, he and Majid were forced to travel by taxi. After prayers at the mosque in Najaf, Majid went to find a driver. He told the driver that, after prayers, the people liked to talk to his father, so that he might have to wait. The driver replied that since he had to wait, he should be paid a hundred fils more than the normal half dinar. Majid agreed to these terms. However, on the way home, his father queried him about the price of the cab. When Majid told him he was paying six hundred fils, his father chided him, telling him that he was paying above the going price for a cab ride from Najaf to Kufa. Majid wanted to know how he knew the cost of a cab ride. His father replied, "I should know how the people live so I ask them about such things."[1]

&

[1] JW: Sayyid 'Abd al-Majid al-Khu'i met a tragic end in 2003, killed by a mob in Kufa when he returned to resume his family's position of leadership. Rumors attributed the murder to Muqtada al-Sadr or his followers, but the matter has never been resolved. See John and Linda Walbridge, "Son of an Ayatollah: Majid al-Khu'i," in Frances Trix, John Walbridge, and Linda S. Walbridge, ed., *Muslim Voices and Lives in the Contemporary World* (New York: Palgrave Macmillan, 2006), pp. 101–11.

Al-Khu'i as Marja' Taqlid

If you ask a devout, observant Shi'ite how he chooses a mujtahid to emulate (to whom to be muqallid), he or she will say that he selects the person most knowledgeable and pious. A mujtahid is a cleric who has not only completed the full course of study at a madrasa (seminary) in Iraq or Iran, but is also recognized by other ulama for his learning and his ability to interpret and make legal judgments independently, based not only on the Qur'an and the life and sayings of the Prophet, but also on the works and behavior of the Imams, whom the Shi'a believe were the rightful heirs of the Prophet. Among these highly trained mujtahids, the Shi'a are supposed to come to a consensus on who best meets the criterion to be the marja' taqlid for the community of believers. It is not permissible to follow a deceased mujtahid. Thus, when a marja' dies, the process of recognizing the most learned mujtahid begins immediately.

For the majority of Shi'a in the world al-Khu'i was the perfect model of the marja' taqlid. His life centered on teaching at the hawza (the academy) in Najaf where he taught more students than any other contemporary mujtahid. In the mornings he read, then travelled from Kufa to Najaf, where he gave lectures, discussed particular religious legal issues with other ulama, responded in writing to the endless questions put to him by Shi'a from all over the world, led prayers, held public majlises, and conferred with the staff who tended to the administration of his offices. His routine varied little and there were continual demands on his time. When not formally engaged in work, there was the endless procession of believers at his door who wanted to bask in the presence of a man so revered that his photograph adorned the homes, mosques, and Husayniyas of Shi'a around the world.

Nor would his routine have varied much from that of the great mujtahids of a hundred or more years ago. Neither would have his style of life, his appearance, or the subjects he taught. He did not value novelty and innovation. He valued the rigors and intricacies of Islamic law and the disciplines associated with it. His method of proving a point was the same as that used by countless generations of his predecessors: questioning others in such a manner that their ignorance would ultimately be revealed and his knowledge and wisdom manifested.

Fadil Jamali referred to his own experience of attending lectures in Najaf, including those of Ayatollah al-Khu'i. He wrote:

> After the intermediate stage the student reaches the third stage of study, which is called the external stage [JW: bahth al-kharij], in which students attend lessons given in public lectures by the Mujtahids. These lectures consist of very highly specialized analysis and examination of religious teachings. Among the famous mujtahids who give such lectures is

Sayyid Muhsin al-Hakim, Sayyid Husain al-Hammani, and Sayyid al-Qasim al-Khu'i. I attended a few of these lectures in December 1957. One of them was al-Khui's lecture in the evening in al-Khadrah Mosque. There were some 150 students attending, all sitting on the ground with legs crossed. The lecture did not last more than thirty minutes. It was on juridical methodology [JW: usul al-fiqh]. I also attended a lecture by Sayyid Husain al-Hammani in the al-Hindi Mosque. Some 150 students were present. The lecture was a on a person's intention or decision, in relationship to prayer. The lecture here had to analyze the meaning of intention and its relation to the act of prayer. The discussion included a great deal of psychology as well. Another lecture I attended was given by Ayatallah Sayyid Muhsin al-Hakim in al-Tusi Mosque. It dealt with the wedding of slaves and the relation of that wedding to the consent of their masters."[2]

There is nothing cutting edge in this curriculum: no modern sciences (the allusion to psychology should not be taken to mean anything resembling the subject matter in a modern university curriculum), no politics, no reference to modern social movements. Al-Khu'i taught the same subjects taught at Najaf generations earlier, and he would have been teaching the same sorts of subjects and with the same methods in the early 1990s as he did in 1957. Yet between 1957 and the early 1990s Iraq underwent upheavals considered cataclysmic even for a part of the world known for its cataclysms. And Najaf was very much at the center of these events.

In 1957 Ayatollah Muhsin al-Hakim, referred to in the paragraph quoted above, was recognized as the marja' taqlid, not Ayatollah al-Khu'i. al-Khu'i, in 1957, was simply a mujtahid qualified to teach at the highest level of the hawza, the "external stage (bahth al-kharij), seminar-style courses in Islamic law. According to his family and others who knew him, he would not have put himself forward as a marja' until after al-Hakim was deceased. Furthermore, Jamali's reference to Hammani suggests that al-Khu'i was not the only mujtahid qualified to teach such courses. Indeed, when al-Khu'i was a young man in the early part of this century, there were thousands of other students. Hanna Batatu notes that there were no fewer than 6,000 students in Najaf in 1918.[3] These would have been al-Khu'i's peers. Were none of them considered eligible to be the marja'? How was it that he actually gained that title? Naturally, while

---

2 Fadil Jamali, "The Theological Colleges of Najaf," *Muslim World* 1960 (50), p. 19.

3 Hanna Batatu, "Shi'i Organizations in Iraq: al-Da'wah al-Islamiyah and al-Mujahidin," in Juan R. I. Cole and Nikki R. Keddie, eds., *Shi'ism and Social Protest,* (New Haven, CT, 1986), p. 189-200.

not all of these students would have gone through the entire educational program of Najaf with its years of study of Islamic law, jurisprudence, Arabic, logic, and philosophy, it can be assumed that a number of them did. Was he so superior to all the others that he automatically became the marja' taqlid?

By the time Fadil Jamali attended lectures, there were only 1954 students in Najaf.[4] Young men were drawn away by the attractions of the modern education provided by the state and by the appeal of occupations in the modern sector, the de-emphasis on sectarian identity, and the popularity of Communist and nationalist ideologies. How did this decrease in numbers of students and the ever-changing political and social scene of Iraq affect the ulama in general and the marja' taqlid in particular?

These questions do not simply relate to Ayatollah al-Khu'i's marja'iya. They are questions central to the institution. What is the real process by which someone becomes recognized as the marja' taqlid and what role does the institution play in the modern world? While there is dispute over the age of the institution of the marja'iya, there is no question that Shi'a have been drawn to the holy cities of Iraq to visit the tombs of the Imams and to study in the madrasas for a thousand years, more than enough time for complex social, political, and theological issues and relationships to have become interwoven. Consequently, the answers to these questions cannot be simple.

The Roots of the Imamate and the Successors of the Imams

The imamate is almost as old as Islam itself. It grew out of the dispute over the succession to the Prophet Muhammad. When he died, the leadership of the community followed a traditional Arab pattern: the community at large formed a consensus that the most senior and respected follower of the Prophet would assume the role of khalifa, or caliph, of the young but expanding religious community. Yet, there were those who argued that the cousin and son-in-law of the Prophet, 'Ali ibn Abi Talib, should assume the role since they were convinced that this is what the Prophet had expressly wished. Two other men ascended to the rank of caliph before 'Ali had his turn, and his reign was to be short-lived. By the time of his recognition as temporal and spiritual leader of the Muslims, there were already sharp divisions in the community, which had now expanded from the far corners of Iran in the east to Egypt in the west. 'Ali was killed by a group of extremists who wanted nothing to do with his conciliatory ways. Mu'awiya, governor of Syria and cousin to 'Ali's

[4] Jamali, "Colleges," p. 15.

predecessor, assumed leadership of the Muslim world and established a government long on bureaucratic know-how but short on religious and spiritual values.

'Ali and his wife, Fatima, the only surviving child of the Prophet, had two sons, Hasan and Husayn. Hasan, with no other choice, accepted the reign of Mu'awiya, passively residing in Medina, Arabia, where his grandfather had established himself as the Messenger of God. With the death of Hasan and the powerful Mu'awiya, Hasan's younger brother, Husayn, urged on by those loyal to the family of the Prophet, decided to make a stand for his rightful place as leader of the Muslims. Accompanied by his family and a small band of supporters, he headed east with the intention of meeting up with supporters who had promised to fight with him. But his supporters had been turned back by the government, and Husayn and his followers were trapped on the edge of the desert, suffering miserably from heat and lack of water. Though fighting fiercely, they were defeated after ten days, and the head of Husayn was delivered to the caliph, Mu'awiya's son Yazid. Husayn was buried in the desert market town of Karbala, about fifty miles north of Najaf, where his father is believed to be buried. This is not the heroic story of victory and conquest that the majority of Muslims in the world remember from the early days of their faith. It is an episode that most would like to forget. However, it is the central collective memory of a significant minority of Muslims, the Shi'a.

'Ali, Hasan, and Husayn are immortalized as the first three Imams of Shi'ism. Those who believe that there is a clear succession of nine more Imams—all descendents of Imam 'Ali and Fatima through Husayn—are referred to as the Ithna-'Ashari, Imami, or Twelver Shi'a. It is out of the institution of the imamate that the Shi'i ulama emerged. Many of the ulama never achieve the high social status of a mujtahid. Instead, with only a limited education behind them, they become the mullas ministering to the needs of a local community or the khatibs who preach and lead the ritual mourning services relating to the suffering of the Imams. The mujtahids are at the top of this social/religious hierarchy. (The word Ayatollah, "sign of God," is a modern title referring to a mujtahid who has attained a significant degree of respect from his peers.) Having completed all three levels of their hawza education, they also have been recognized as qualified to make independent judgments on disputed points of Islamic law and to act as representatives of the Imam. The marja' taqlid, the "source of emulation," is at the pinnacle of this hierarchy.

In this book we will be looking at the modern institution of the marja'iya: what men must do or, for that matter, avoid doing to become a marja', what it means to be a marja', how the institution is sustained, its function in the modern world, and its relationship with governments, lower-ranking ulama, and the laity.

Chapter 2

The Passing of the Mantle

AN 'ALIM OF A PRESTIGIOUS FAMILY from Karbala tells that when the marja' Sayyid Mahdi Shirazi died, he was to be buried in Karbala. Muhsin al-Hakim was the grand marja' in Najaf at the time. Al-Hakim, who reportedly was a friend of Shirazi, went to Karbala to show his respect and to pray over his body. The most prominent mujtahid would be expected to do so. While al-Hakim waited in a room for the body to be prepared, someone announced over the loudspeaker that it had been the will of Mahdi Shirazi that his thirty-year-old son, Muhammad, would lead the prayers. Al-Hakim's followers at the funeral were furious and urged al-Hakim to leave. In their eyes this was a terrible insult to Ayatollah al-Hakim .

This story and subsequent events regarding Sayyid Muhammad Shirazi are a part of Iraqi Shi'i history that everyone seems to want to forget. Yet the life and times of Muhammad Shirazi are critical for understanding the modern marja'iya. The picture of Muhammad Shirazi varies with the person portraying him. He is either hero or villain, grand propagator of Shi'ism or radical divisive force.

First, though, we should see what this funeral situation tells us about the marja'iya. Ayatollah Mahdi Shirazi, a man known more for his piety than for his learning, wanted his son, Muhammad, to fill his role in Karbala. Praying over his body at his funeral would focus attention on his son, a means used commonly to advance someone's marja'iya. There are other ways of doing this, as well. For example, it is common practice for the ulama to send letters of condolence on the occasion of the death of a marja' to the person they believe is his likely successor. That person, then, will be expected to pray over the body of the deceased marja' if he wishes to publicly establish that he wishes to be recognized as a marja'. However, simply having the quiet support of other ulama does not guarantee that one will be recognized universally as the marja'.

While al-Hakim's followers were very angry at what they deemed an insult to their marja', this incident did no damage to al-Hakim's standing. Al-Hakim's position by then was well established, and his followers were spread far and wide. Yet the incident proved to be significant nevertheless. It was the beginning of a quest for leadership that was ultimately denied to Muhammad Shirazi. In this funeral service, one can see how the seeds of his undoing were sown. Had the matter ended with the funeral, more than likely relations between him and his followers, on the one hand, and the hawza in Najaf on the other would have been smoothed over. As mentioned above, his father was considered the marja' of Karbala and had cordial relations with the grand marja'— that is, Ayatollah al-Hakim —of Najaf. The roles of the two men seem to have been clearly delineated so that they were not in competition with one another.

It was apparent soon after the funeral that Muhammad Shirazi was not content with simply taking on the role that his father had carved out for himself. That Muhammad Shirazi aspired to be more than the leading mujtahid of Karbala is attested by the fact that his wakils, representatives, travelled around Iraq, even to the Sunni provinces, promoting him, in an obvious attempt to combine religious prestige with political clout, referring to him as "al-Imam al-Mujaddid," the renewing imam.[5] They also went to Najaf to loudly proclaim Shirazi as the grand marja' of the time, which was a source of considerable irritation to the hawza of Najaf. For one thing, the grand marja', Ayatollah al-Hakim , was still alive. Equally important was the fact that one does not build his marja'iya in such a fashion. However, it was not the al-Hakim-Shirazi relationship that was the most affected by the activities of the Shirazi followers. After all, Ayatollah al-Hakim was well established, and no one could compete with him. It was those rising to prominence after the death of Ayatollah al-Hakim who would find Shirazi's ambitions particularly trying.

Yet, this is not a simple matter of competition. There was something extremely unusual about Shirazi's quest for the marja'iya. He was far too young and inexperienced to be a marja'. As one person said, "He did not even have a white beard to recommend him." Implicit in this statement is

[5] JW: This refers to a tradition, recognized both by Sunnis and Shi'a, that in every century there will be a religious scholar who will renew Islam. Various eminent scholars are identified as the "mujaddid," renewer, of one century or another.

the fact that he had not risen through the ranks of the hawza following the traditional procedure for becoming a marja'. He had set himself outside of the system, yet was aspiring for a role that was clearly within the system.

Muhammad Shirazi's career in Iraq did not last long. His political activities drew the attention of the Ba'thist government. When word reached him that he was to be arrested, he left for Kuwait. Twenty-five of his followers were not so fortunate and were imprisoned. An old friend of Shirazi, Sayyid Murtada Musawi Qazwini, received a warning from a government official that he too would be arrested if he did not leave immediately. The night of the warning he and his family left for Kuwait. Also, among those in the Shirazi entourage who escaped were his two nephews Hadi and Muhammad-Taqi Mudarrisi, to whom we will refer later.

In Kuwait Shirazi was free to pursue his goals. According to one of the sons of Sayyid Murtada Qazwini, Mustafa Qazwini, Shirazi was very active and did a remarkable job of attracting people to religious activity. The number of Shi'i mosques increased by five or six times. The number of Husayniyas increased greatly in the 1970s. These latter are meeting places for recounting the sufferings of the Imams, important for spreading the reputation of charismatic preachers. Youth who had not been attending mosque began to do so. Shirazi made visits to prominent people and encouraged them to participate in the political and economic life of the country. He encouraged the Kuwaiti Shi'a to publish magazines and the young people to become political writers. A flurry of intellectual, religious, and political activity during the 1970s led to an Islamic revival. Indeed, the young Shirazi along with his dedicated band of followers, while perhaps appearing as the archetypal scourge of the West, might have been considered the models of modern Shi'ism.

The 1970s were also a time when Ayatollah al-Khu'i, the most obvious successor to al-Hakim , was establishing his marja'iya. He had, after all, more students in the hawza than perhaps any other mujtahid had ever had. As one informant, a person who had been muqallid to al-Khu'i throughout the Ayatollah's reign as marja', said, "The al-Khu'is [meaning his family and followers] believed that they were entitled to the marja'iya." Therefore, they did not look favorably upon Shirazi's activities in Kuwait.

The situation was intensified by the fact that Shirazi's brother Hasan, a jurist himself, had become popular in Lebanon and had good relations with the press, which portrayed him as being comparable with al-Khu'i. Shirazi's picture began to appear a great deal in Lebanon. A person from a group in Kuwait opposed to Shirazi asked Ayatollah al-Khu'i if Shirazi was qualified to be a mujtahid. Ayatollah al-Khu'i wrote a fatwa in which he said that Shirazi was not a student of his. How this statement is interpreted depends on the interpreter. Many people read it as damning Shirazi. One informant said that a group of Muslim activists used the fatwa to silence Shirazi followers in the 1980s. Others will say it is a mild and neutral sort of statement, indicating that al-Khu'i simply was not familiar with Shirazi's qualifications. However, in spite of (or perhaps because of) Muhammad Shirazi's activities and the support of his brother Hasan in building his marja'iya in the Gulf and in Lebanon, his fortunes dwindled after al-Khu'i's statement about him.

There was another rising star in Najaf as well, the late Muhammad-Baqir al-Sadr, whose legacy as a religious and political leader lives on. That his relations with Shirazi were, if anything, even more antagonistic than those between al-Khu'i and Shirazi is evident. After all, Baqir al-Sadr and Shirazi were both breaking out of the quietest ulama role and were determined to shape the politics of the region. More will be said about Baqir al-Sadr, including his relations with Shirazi, in chapter five

Shirazi's life was to take a sharp turn in the late 1970s with the onset of the Iranian Revolution. Whether he felt pushed to go to Iran because of the "condemnation" of Ayatollah al-Khu'i, or whether he was simply caught up in the optimism of the Iranian Revolution cannot be determined. We know that Shirazi was a political activist and that he had developed a friendship with Khomeini, the latter having stayed with him as his guest for ten days in Karbala. Furthermore, he gave his place as the leader of prayers to Khomeini at that time. Obviously, some obligations had been established, and Shirazi and his followers decided to throw in their lot with the revolutionaries in Iran. They continued to play a role in the great drama that lay ahead, but that will be told later.

For now, it is important to point out that the incident involving Shirazi's quest for the marja'iya intensified the longstanding poor relations between Najaf, where the Imam 'Ali is buried, and Karbala, where the remains of the Imam Husayn are interred. Competition between the two cities for the pilgrim traffic was been intense in the twentieth century. Karbala is often referred to as a city with a large Iranian population, while Najaf is frequently portrayed as "Arab." This is probably an oversimplification. Many Iranians were drawn to Karbala, but they also intermarried with Arabs. The Iranians have left their cultural mark on Karbala, but in this region it is difficult to sort out ethnicity and nationality. Al-Khu'i was Iranian. He lived in Najaf, and while he sent his sons to a Persian-speaking school, his sons identified themselves as Iraqis. Whatever the ethnic and cultural differences, certainly a primary factor in the dynamics of the region has been political hostilities between the governments of Iran and Iraq.[6] However, one spin that has been placed on the recent rivalry between Karbala and Najaf is that the people of Karbala, especially of the merchant class, were eager to have an "Iranian" marja' replace Ayatollah al-Hakim , who was looked upon as an "Arab" marja'. However, this does not explain the rivalry between Shirazi and al-Khu'i, as both could be considered Iranian.

Shirazi's move to Iran removed any threat that he may have had to al-Khu'i's marja'iya. Until his death in 1992, Ayatollah al-Khu'i remained in Najaf, where he continued to write, respond to questions, lead prayers, and gain in worldwide prestige. If one talks to the rank-and-file Shi'a, one would be left with the impression that Ayatollah al-Khu'i's inheritance of the marja'iya was so natural that there could have been no question at all as to its occurrence. However, those close to the marja' know the story a bit differently. Aside from Shirazi, there was al-Hakim 's own son, Yusuf, who was a possible candidate. More formidable competition came from the above-mentioned cleric, Muhammad-Baqir al-Sadr and from Ayatollah Khomeini. How did Ayatollah al-Khu'i gain so much prestige? One of his relatives has said that it was not "logical" that al-Khu'i should be the marja' because "he was so scholarly and unambitious. There was pressure on him to become a marja'." This statement is indeed a very telling one. Hidden in it lies the answers to some key questions about the nature of the marja'iya.

Attempting to define the Marja'iya

Thus far we have been speaking about the marja'iya as if it were a tangible sort of office, something very clearly defined. Certainly when one talks to those who are muqallid to a marja' it is easy to be left with such an impression. The followers of the marja' seek this leading jurist's rulings on a wide range of behaviors and rituals. As Khuri (has written:

> Implicit in the principle of "interpretation" is the belief that all proper behavior can be derived from Islamic tradition, which imposes upon the convert a constant obligation to know the official religious stand on the day-to-day activities of life. If he is ignorant of the intrinsic meaning of the revealed text and lacks the specialized skills to derive laws of conduct from tradition, the layman should follow the behavior of those who have a claim to knowledge—the learned men.[7]

The person who follows the marja', the muqallid, also pays part of his

---

[6] Yitzhak Nakash, *The Shi'is of Iraq* (Princeton: Princeton University Press, 1994).

[7] Fu'ād I. Khūrī, *Tribe and State in Bahrain: The Transformation of Social and Political Authority in an Arab State* (Publications of the Center for Middle Eastern Studies 14. Chicago: University of Chicago Press, 1980), p. 71.

religious tax to the marja'. The most important Shi'a religious tax is the khums (one fifth of a person's net income). In Shi'ism the ulama rely on the laymen for support, whereas the Sunni ulama base their affairs on donations from the government. These arrangements reflect the different roles that the ulama of the two sects play in society. The Sunni ulama are seen as supporting the state, while the Shi'a conduct their affairs outside of the domain of government and are often at odds with the rulers.[8]

While the issue of the payment of khums and its use have been subjects of debate among Shi'i scholars throughout the centuries, the present day interpretation, as given by Ayatollah Hakim, is that

> a well-qualified mujtahid in the religious sciences could act as the representative (wakil, na'ib) of the imam and collect the khums on his behalf. This na'ib had to be the most learned (al-a'lam) and righteous (al-'adil) jurist. Both these conditions were desirable in a mujtahid to ensure the proper use of the khums in accordance with the imam in occultation. The mujtahid, having received the khums, was to divide it into two parts: the sahm al-Imam and the sahm al-sadat. The first portion, the portion which includes the three shares of God, the Prophet, and the imam, was to be used for the propagation of the faith and other similar activities. . . The other portion, namely, sahm al-sadat, was to be distributed strictly among the Banu Hashim.[9]

The reference to the portion for the "Banu Hashim" refers to the payment given to the sayyids, the descendents of the Prophet. The money is to go only to poor sayyids. (If it were otherwise, then the marja' could be entitled to the entire khums, as the majority of maraji' are sayyids.) The payment of the khums concretizes the relationship between the marja' and those muqallid to him. However, even with the khums, the marja'iya tends to be a rather ephemeral institutions in many respects.

Western scholars have attempted to nail down the inauguration of the institution. Historians such as Juan Cole and Abbas Amanat have argued that the institution of the marja'iya resulted from competition between the Akhbari and the Usuli schools in the eighteenth century.[10] The Akhbaris believed that scripture and tradition from past generations pro-

---

8 For some interesting comparisons between the way Shi'a and Sunni communities operate, see Khuri, *Tribe,* and Fu'ād Isḥāq Khūrī, *Imams and Emirs: State, Religion and Sects In Islam* (London: Saqi, 1990).

9 Abdulaziz Abdulhussein Sachedina, The Just Ruler (al-sultān Al-'ādil) in Shī'ite Islam: The Comprehensive Authority of the Jurist In Imamite Jurisprudence (New York: Oxford University Press, 1988), p. 244.

10 Juan Cole, "Imami Jurisprudence"; Abbas Amanat, *Resurrection and Renewal: The Making of the Babi Movement in Iran,* 1844–1850 (Ithaca, NY: Cornell University Press, 1989), p. 34 ff.

vided the only source for forming legal judgments. In other words, they were opposed to ijtihad—the use of deductive reasoning and the principles of jurisprudence, usul al-fiqh,[11] to arrive at judgments.) The Usulis, on the other hand, gave the mujtahids far more leeway (and power) in forming judgments. This school promoted the use of ijtihad, which was the sole province of those who had the training and skills (i.e., the mujtahids) to deduce facts from the Qur'an and the traditions. As Amanat explains,

> . . . by defining the terms and conditions of ijtihad and by recognizing the superior intellectual and moral advantages of mujtahids, the Usulis designated themselves a religious elite entitled to rights and priorities above others, and most of all to moral leadership of the community.[12]

The Usuli ulama came not only to control most aspects of the law including civil and commercial courts, but also to convince lay Shi'a that they should emulate mujtahids in the way that they would the Twelve Imams.

In contrast to the argument that the marja'iya is a relatively new phenomenon, Shi'i scholars themselves argue that the institution of the marja'iya dates back to the Occultation of the Twelfth Imam in the ninth century. A list provided by an Iraqi religious scholar cites thirty-one individuals who were considered to be maraji' prior to Shaykh Muhammad Hasan Najafi (1786-1850), the author of the famous work *al-Jawahir*, whom Elie Kedourie[13] cites as the first recognized marja'. However, they will concede that with the advent of better means of communication, such as the telegraph, the institution became more centralized. It became increasingly possible for one person to be acclaimed by all as having unquestionable prominence. To him all Shi'a would turn for instruction on every matter relating to one's spiritual and ritual duty, and to him Shi'a would send their tithes.

Baqir al-Sadr, the Iraqi scholar and activist who was executed in Iraq in 1980, saw the marja'iya has being divided into four historical stages, increasing in each stage in terms of centralization and consolidation. His

---

[11] JW: Usul al-fiqh is an elaborate discipline that attempts to codify the ways in which rules governing new legal cases may be deduced from the Qur'an, the sayings and reports handed down from the Prophet, early generations of believers, and, in the case of the Shi'a, the Imams. It deals with such questions as the proper analysis of language, the use of analogy, degrees of obligation, and contradictory evidence. It is taught only to the advanced students in the madrasas.

[12] Amanat, *Resurrection*, p. 37.

[13] Elie Kedourie, "The Iraqi Shi'is and Their Fate," in Martin Kramer, ed. *Shi'ism Resistence and Revolution* (Boulder, CO: Westview, 1987). pp. 135-157.

first stage begins with the period of the Imams and continues until 'Allama al-Hilli's development of the role of the mujtahid in the fourteenth century. His "central marja'iya," beginning in the eighteenth century, corresponds to the Western scholars' dating of the beginning of the marja'iya. Baqir al-Sadr's fourth stage, the "popular marja'iya," refers to the direct involvement of the marja' in politics against imperialism, an idea not universally accepted, but one that will be discussed at length later.[14]

There is no doubt that the late eighteenth century was a watershed for the Shi'i establishment. At that time the leadership of the ulama appears to have been obvious. Aqa Muhammad-Baqir Bihbahani had gained such prominence as the major proponent of the successful Usuli School that he was acknowledged by scholars both in Iran and Iraq as "the master of all."[15] After his death in 1791 no one individual appears to have had the prestige of Bihbahani, and it was not until the mid-1840s that a mujtahid arose again as the highest source of emulation. However, Bihbahani set the stage for the modern marja'iya.

It is important to this discussion to examine how the position of the marja' has been filled in the past, or at least how it is perceived as having been filled. Cole (1983) has written that the highly influential marja', Murtada Ansari, was appointed by his predecessor, Shaykh Muhammad Hasan. Cole believes that Shaykh Hasan's move to appoint a successor was probably an attempt to "formalize the selection of the new source for emulation and to make that selection the prerogative of the preceding holder of the post."[16] Ansari himself, who taught that emulation of a marja' was required of all lay Shi'is, expounded on the position of the marja' and, in the process, laid the major portion of responsibility for selection of the marja' with the layperson himself. Ansari, according to Cole, stated that the layperson may depend on the advice of a "just man" who is an expert on the law, or on the advice of a group of experts. Should he wish to identify a mujtahid who is not considered the most learned, then he "must seek the advice of at least two just men who are experts."[17] Ultimately, no formal process for designation was established. As Lambton states,

---

14 "The Islamic Political Theory of Muhammad-Baqir al-Sadr." Dissertation, University of Utah, 1991.

15 Amanat, *Resurrection,* pp. 35–37.

16 Juan R. I. Cole, "Imami Jurisprudence and the Role of the Ulama: Murtaza Ansari on Emulating the Supreme Exemplar," in Nikki R. Keddie, ed., *Religion and Politics in Iran: Shi'ism from Quietism to Revolution* (New Haven: Yale University Press, 1983), p. 41.

17 Cole, "Imami Jurisprudence," p. 43.

> Certain qualifications were stipulated with regard to (the marja' al-taqlid's) person but there was no form of election: in due course he 'emerged' and became known to all, and was acknowledged by the general consensus. There was no way in which this acknowledgement received explicit expression, but it nevertheless became known in due course and was accepted by the body of believers.[18]

As we shall see later, since the 1960s the issue of formalizing the selection problem has been a major concern of various Shi'i groups. Whether or not to formalize it and, if so, how the community would go about it is a major source of contention among the Shi'a today.

Returning to Ansari's interpretation of the layman's role in the selection process, it seems only fair to ask, how exactly this is this "emergence" supposed to occur? While it may not seem unreasonable to expect a lay person to consult with two people who are 'adil (trustworthy) before deciding which marja' to follow or, alternatively, to consult a mujtahid who is muhtat (practices precaution)—a high ranking mujtahid who has not put himself forward as a marja' himself—there are many who do not follow one of these two prescribed paths. Individuals, unless they are accustomed to close contact with the ulama, generally do not seek such guidance. Shi'a commonly remark that they simply "know" whom to follow based on the mujtahid's fame and what others around them are doing. It would seem that such a method would tend to negate the notion of one supreme exemplar. Indeed, Michael Fischer mentions that in 1975 there were "six first-rank maraji'-i taqlid: al-Khoi and Khomeyni in Najaf; Golpaygani, Shari'atmadari, and Marashi-Najafi in Qom; Khonsari in Tehran."[19] Fischer also remarks that "the term, (i.e., marja'-i taqlid). . . is also used more loosely to refer to people who administer the several hawza-i 'ilmi (learning centers), who give out student stipends, and who thereby are really patrons."[20] Fischer observed (in the 1970s) that the theory of the marja'iya seems not to have been firmly established. Yet, throughout the past couple of hundred years, there are mujtahids who have been referred to, by both Western scholars and Shi'a, as the "sole marja" of the Shi'i world, giving the term an aura of an institution firmly embedded and universally recognized and revered in the community, similar to the papacy in Roman Catholicism.

Certainly, the term "sole marja'" is somewhat misleading. As Cole

---

[18] Ann K. S. Lambton, "A Reconsideration of the Postion of the Marja' al-Taqlid and the Religious Institution," *Studia Islamica* 20 (1964), p. 119.

[19] Michael M. J. Fischer, *Iran: From Religious Dispute to Revolution* (Harvard Studies in Cultural Anthrolopogy 3; Cambridge: Harvard University Press, 1980), p. 88.

[20] Fischer, *Iran,* p. 88.

points out, "in the mid-nineteenth century each of the major centers of Shi'i learning possessed one or two leading mujtahids," but in the 1840s Najaf become preeminent.[21] According to Moussavi (1994) that the efforts of Shaykh Muhammad Hasan Najafi to consolidate the Shi'ite centers and introduce "a capable successor (Ansari) for his position, indicates that he was aware of the institutional functions which devolved upon the *marja'iya*."[22] The preeminence of Najaf came into question in the 1920s when the Qom hawza was established and the ulama of Najaf were living in exile in Iran. Judging from the way the marja' taqlid is determined and by the ambiguity that seems to surround the position, is it really possible to have a sole marja'? What the world may have is a grand marja' who has the greatest following throughout the world, while there still may be room for lesser maraji'. Simply because this is how the marja'iya has tended to operate does not mean that it is completely acceptable to the muqallid. The fact that the marja'iya cannot be "pinned down" and very precisely defined is disturbing to Shi'a thinkers who wish to see the institution revamped. This is a theme we will take up later.

Speaking in a very general and idealistic sense, the person who is seeking to make taqlid should look for the person who best combines the qualities of learning and reason with those of extreme piety and devotion and a "fair and just character."[23] Ann Lambton in her discussion of the emergence of the marja' taqlid, emphasizes the precedence that knowledge has over any other quality.[24] As the representative of the "general deputyship" of the Imam, the marja', or source of emulation, must be capable of performing the duel role of chief legal expert and spiritual model for the community of believers. He must possess a very high level of knowledge of fiqh and usul al-fiqh (Islamic law and the principles of its deduction respectively) that should be reflected in his teaching and his writings. These characteristics are not easily translated into testable, quantifiable terms.

Some mujtahids and intellectuals have seen the role of the marja' as more broadly defined than that of a purely religious scholar. In this century the Shi'i world has hotly debated the role of religious leaders in worldly affairs. Murtada Mutahhari, for example, whose writings were

---

[21] Juan R. I. Cole, Sacred Space and Holy War: The Politics, Culture and History of Shi'ite Islam (London: I. B. Tauris, 2002), p. 92.

[22] Ahmad Kazemi Moussavi, "The Institutionalization of Marja'-i Taqlid in the Nineteenth Century Shi'ite Community," *The Muslim World* 84/3-4 (1994), p. 289.

[23] Kazemi Mousavi, "Insitutionalization," p. 291.

[24] Lambton, "Reconsideration," pp. 121–22.

highly influential in revolutionary Iran, considered it a paramount duty of lay Shi'a to act responsibly in choosing a righteous leader to follow. He also rejects "the followership of a deceased religious authority," insisting on "the necessity of choosing a living exemplary model to emulate. . . because the changing conditions of the world demand a living tradition and its supreme figures of authority."[25] How responsive the marja' is supposed to be to changing social and political conditions is a debate that plays out at all levels of religious leadership and permeates discussions on a vast array of topics.

Regardless of the political views of a mujtahid and how he perceives himself in terms of his role in society, if he is putting himself forward as a marja', he will be expected by those seeking to make taqlid to have produced a legal manual (risala) summarizing his legal opinions without giving the elaborate proofs required in legal manuals written for the ulama. It is assumed that if he does not produce one, then he is not putting himself forward as a candidate for the marja'iya. In a number of cases I have heard people close to the senior ulama claim that a particular mujtahid was well qualified in their view to be a marja' but that person did not write a risala, making it clear to them that this person did not seek the role. Ordinary lay people also expect that a marja' would have a risala. Yet it was not until after Sayyid Muhammad Kazim Tabataba'i Yazdi, the author of *al-'Urwa al-Wuthqa*, who died in 1918, that it became customary for each marja' to write such a treatise. It is his risala that is the template for all others, and all the contenders to the marja'iya footnote it with their own opinions.

Topics addressed in a risala are consistent regardless of the author. The risala, since the time of Yazdi, has been in two parts. The first part deals with ritual, including such subjects as the kinds of prayer and what is necessary to make it acceptable to God, modesty, fasting, and ritual cleanliness. This is the part of the risala most often spoken about and most often referred to. The Shi'a have a far more ritualistic life than do the Sunnis. Their emphasis on ritual activities and ritual purity is very much a result of the fact that they have lived as a persecuted or at least marginalized group on the periphery of Muslim society throughout most of their history. Only in Iran have they gained dominance. The second part of the risala deals with "transactions," be they personal or business. Rules about marriage and divorce are included in this part of the risala and are referred to more than any of the other rules in this category.

---

[25] Hamid Dabashi, Theology of Discontent: The Ideological Foundation of the Islamic Revolution in Iran (New York: New York University Press, 1993), p. 164.

Though content of the risala is directed to the layman, the linguistic style is far from colloquial. Still, the risala does not have to be written in Arabic; if the mujtahid's native tongue is Persian, for example, the risala can be written in that language. The risala tells the believer what is licit (halal), recommended, indifferent, discouraged, and forbidden (haram). The risala of one marja' might say that a particular food is haram, while another might say it is simply discouraged. This is generally as radical a difference in opinion as can be found among the various risalas of the maraji'. This is not surprising since bid'a (innovation) is forbidden. There is some variation in opinions regarding the degree to which a woman must be covered, but these differences are subtle and not easily discernible to someone outside the system. Differences in exactly how one should perform his ablutions (wudu') before praying, precisely how to define sunset during Ramadan (should one wait an additional fifteen minutes after the sun has set to break the fast as a matter of precaution?), and other such details differentiate the teachings of one marja' from another.

Since the risalas of the maraji' generally do not differ significantly and since the risala is perhaps the only text of the marja' that a follower might even look at, it may seem at this point puzzling that so much emphasis goes into selecting the "correct" marja'. Yet the authors of the risalas are adamant that following the right marja' is a grave matter, so much so that the person who follows the "wrong" one is left in doubt as to whether even his prayers will be acceptable to God, for, according to the writings of the maraji', it is only by performing one's prayers and ablutions absolutely correctly, only by keeping the fast totally within the prescribed bounds, and only by avoiding everything that is possibly impure (najis) that one can be assured that he is abiding by the will of God.

Matters not covered by a risala can also be addressed by the marja'. On such matters, the marja' answers on a case-by-case basis and does not make sweeping generalities based on such cases. Aside from the risala, the marja' is expected to devote considerable amounts of time expounding religious legal matters. Using a pen and ink, he will spend endless hours producing dozens of volumes of manuscripts that are, these days, put to print and published. The topics are standard and more or less identical to those in the risalas, though unlike the risalas, they are likely to be accompanied by arguments and proofs. Yet, these are volumes that will probably not be read by anyone other than other ulama and their students. These resolutely pedantic writings will not generally sway the average Shi'ite to become muqallid to a particular mujtahid. Other means have to be put into action.

After the Death of a Marja'

What happens when a marja' dies? Can the muqallid continue to follow the teachings of the dead marja' or does he have to choose a living marja'? For the Usuli Shi'a, the usual answer to this question is that the Shi'a are always supposed to follow a living marja', but there actually is not a clear-cut answer to this question. The maraji' themselves disagree on this matter. Ayatollah Yazdi, whose risala has become the model for all others, permitted the muqallid to remain with the dead marja'. Others challenge this notion. The general consensus is that one can follow the teachings of the dead marja' until he stumbles upon a new issue that needs to be addressed. Once the new marja' is consulted, he should make taqlid to that marja' and not return to the old one. One might well ask how often the average Shi'ite is going to come across a new issue that needs an answer. Considering that a majority of Shi'a might never need the answer to any new religious question, what keeps most people from simply continuing to follow a dead marja'? There are multiple answers to this question and they are all interlinked. Ultimately, these can be summed up in the comment of one person: "It is part of Shi'i culture to find a new marja'."

The quest for the new marja' is a never-ending drama played out in various parts of the world and with many actors. There are subtleties to this drama that can only be appreciated on very close inspection. These subtleties frequently are very consequential and can shape the direction of the institution.

Returning briefly to the topic of Ayatollah Shirazi's death, we can begin to understand some of the actual processes of the succession of power. Whether or not the scholarly literature refers to Shirazi as a marja', in the eyes of those who were muqallid to him, he was one. In his case, those who were muqallid to him would have been people directly connected to him in Karbala. Shirazi is what has become known as a "local marja'." His reputation and influence were quite limited, especially in comparison to the leading marja' residing in Iraq, Ayatollah Muhsin al-Hakim of Najaf. While Muhsin al-Hakim was referred to as a "grand marja'," this did not preclude Shirazi, or even mujtahids in Najaf, from being paid khums and writing risalas.

Muhammad Shirazi would have seen a window of opportunity open for himself at the death of his father. If he, rather than al-Hakim, prayed at the funeral of his father, especially when al-Hakim was in Karbala at the same time, this would have sent a message to those who saw or heard about the event, that al-Hakim was deferring to Shirazi. Such deferential treatment could suggest that al-Hakim wanted Shirazi to succeed him as grand marja' or even that he saw him as more or less an equal. At the least, it would have signaled that Muhammad Shirazi was a person the Shi'a should pay close attention to, a statement that he was a strong contender in the quest for the marja'iya.

The fact is that there were others—men who resided in Najaf at the same time as Al-Hakim—who also had claims to being the future grand marja'. Ayatollah al-Khu'i was one of these. In the following chapters we will see how Ayatollah al-Khu'i and others have risen to the station of grand marja'. In the process, we will examine the roles of those who do not—or have not yet—been considered grand marja', as these men may indeed be important players in the drama.

Chapter Three

Sons and Students: Spreading the Reputation of the Marja'

SAYYID MURTADA QAZWINI was being introduced as a speaker at a mosque one evening in Los Angeles. The person introducing him commented that, as an indicator of his success in life, two of his sons were sitting in the audience. Sayyid Qazwini corrected the man. "Four of my sons are in the audience," he stated with apparent pride. He added that he had never felt stronger now that all six of his sons were either living with him or close by him.

AS THE STORY CITED ABOVE INDICATES, one of the reasons Muhammad Shirazi was considered an upstart when he made his bid for the marja'iya was that he was so young at the time: merely in his thirties. Ideally, a marja' taqlid should be at least twice this age. Not only should the marja' have the highest character and greatest degree of learning, but he must also look like a marja'. His hair and long beard should be white, his countenance serious, even stern, his abaya (robe) preferably a bit shopworn. The Middle East is known for revering its patriarchs. The marja' taqlid should be the generous, modest, austere, benevolent, wise, severe, saintly patriarch par excellence. He also distinguishes himself in other ways. For example, he usually does not give speeches, only advice. He typically does not wear a watch, nor the high clerical collar that lower-ranking ulama wear. He sits on the floor, not on a chair.

While a man with these characteristics and behaviors may be the ideal, he is not the sort of person who is likely to draw a great deal of attention to himself. This scholarly, elderly individual who is admired for the humility of his lifestyle and his avoidance of worldliness must somehow connect with the rest of the Shi'i world. People must learn about him. Even in Iraq in the vicinity of the shrine cities—even in the shrine cities themselves—there are Shi'a who need to be informed about the importance of the marja'iya in general and the mujtahids qualified for this position in particular. Certainly not all Shi'a felt it to be one of the urgencies of their lives to select a marja' and pay religious tax to him. One informant said that, when he was growing up in Iraq in the 1960s, his father was very devoted to Ayatollah al-Hakim and used to go to Najaf himself to pay his khums to him. A friend of this informant considered it noteworthy that this family had a large photograph of al-Hakim in their home and was aware that they were unusually religious for the time, especially for urban and educated people. If such an effort was needed to reach local people, how much more would be needed to reach people abroad? How does the marja' entice the believers to refer to his own risala and to pay their religious tax to him? The answer essentially is that he does not. The Shi'a do not want a marja' who appears to be too eager for the role. The comment cited above that Ayatollah al-Khu'i had been pressured to become a marja' is what one would expect to hear from a devotee of a marja'. Abrahamian, writing about Ayatollah Khomeini, who also was considered a marja' taqlid, says very much the same thing:

> (His students) had to plead with him (Khomeini) to get him to publish his *Towzih al-Masa'el* [Khomeini's risala] so that he would be recognized by others as a grand ayatollah. They quoted him as saying that he preferred to remain a 'humble teacher and scholar.' They claim that when Ayatollah Al-Hakim, another senior cleric, died in 1970, Khomeini again ordered his followers not to campaign on his behalf for the title of supreme marja-e taqlid. For his disciples, this modesty proved not only that Khomeini was a man of the people but also that he possessed the prerequisite quality needed to lead the Islamic community.[26]

It should be noted here that Ayatollah Khomeini began his risala while in Turkey, even before he had gone to Iraq.[27] The writing of the

---

26 Ervand Abrahamian, *Khomeinism: Essays on the Islamic Republic.* (Berkeley: University of California Press, 1993), p. 50.

27 JW: Khomeini wrote two risalas: *Tahrir al-Wasila,* written in Arabic, and *Tawdih al-Masa'il* in Persian. The former was written, or perhaps begun, while he was in Turkey in 1964, but the bibliographic history of these works seems somewhat confused; see Dabashi, *Theology,* pp. 411, 429. The latter is translated by J. Borujerdi, *A Clarification of Questions* (Boulder: Westview, 1984).

risala is a definite sign that one wishes to be a marja'. However, while the writing of a risala is acceptable, preaching to the masses that one is aspiring to be a marja' is not.

If the marja' himself is hindered from spreading the word about his marja'iya, who can do so? While the marja''s students and former students bear some of the responsibility, this is not the entire picture. Of paramount importance to the marja' is his hierarchical network of representatives, at the top of which are his sons and sons-in-law. The importance of sons and sons-in-law to the marja'iya is difficult to overestimate. They are commonly referred to, only half-jokingly, as the marja''s "chiefs of staff" and as his "eyes and ears." Usually trained in the madrasas themselves, they frequently do not come close to attaining their father's high religious status. It is unusual for the son of a marja' to become a marja' himself, though there are exceptions. The case of Muhammad Shirazi's quest for the marja'iya after the death of his father indicates that some ulama do desire to follow in their fathers' illustrious footsteps. However, it is more likely that the son will have a background in the religious sciences, but also develop organizational and political skills that prove far more advantageous to advancing his father's position than if he too focused simply on religious education. As I have been told repeatedly, it takes time to build up one's marja'iya. It also takes know-how and savvy, at least on the part of the key supporters of the marja'.

The marja' himself is supposed to be the elderly scholar/saint, regardless of whether he has a militant position on politics or removes himself from such worldly debates. He has a particular charisma that comes with conforming to the image of the scholar saint, (though, as Cole and Ashraf explain, charisma can belong to the marja' himself or to the institution of the marja'iya, a subject which we will address later.[28]) For our purposes at the moment, however, the *marja'* will be, as one 'alim put it, "good, pious, and humble," and it should not be anticipated that such a person will be adroit at announcing himself as the best candidate for the *marja'iya.* As a matter of fact, if he is adroit in this way, he should hide this ability, as such qualities are looked upon as highly undesirable in the *marja'*. However, others must be able to advertise his position. In a patrilineal society, who better to fulfill this role than the marja''s sons? The bond of loyalty and trust should be strongest between the father and the son. It should be unquestioned. Therefore, we might expect the son to be given great leverage in the way in which his father's marja'iya is conducted.

---

[28] Cole, "Jurisprudence"; Ahmad Ashraf, "Theocracy and Charisma: New Men of Power in Iran," *International Journal of Politics, Culture, and Society* 4/1 (1990), pp. 113-152.

Ahmad Khomeini was notorious for his strong presence in the marja'iya of his father. Informants have said that he would frequently interrupt people who were asking his father for his help or involvement in a matter. Ahmad would chime in with his own answer, generally refusing the request. And there the issue would end. In one account, a fourth party was present during an interaction between Khomeini, Muhammad Shirazi, and Ahmad Khomeini. While Shirazi had been an active supporter of the Iranian Revolution in the early days after the fall of the Shah, he later came to have strong disagreements with the government. As mentioned earlier, Shirazi and Khomeini had established a friendship while Khomeini was in Iraq. However, the differences between them had grown to such a point that they had become estranged, so a mutual friend intervened. Khomeini was hospitalized in Tehran at the time when the mutual friend arranged a meeting between the two men. There were two meetings between Khomeini and Shirazi, and both apparently went well, with the two men appearing to resolve their differences over a political matter. However, during the third meeting, Ahmad Khomeini was present. He positioned himself between Khomeini and Shirazi and said that his father did not become involved in such matters. The discussions ended at that point, with Khomeini acceding to his son's advice. As an 'alim living in the United States said, "Our maraji' have no unseen knowledge. For example, if you have a question, you need sources of information. You go and get the information. It is the same with the marja'. They too need information. Their sons are the nearest ones to them to give them advice and information." Yet it is apparent from the accounts of Ahmad Khomeini that he took the liberty to do much more than just pass on information to his father. He obviously assumed the role the Khomeini's followers believed belonged solely to the grand ayatollah himself. One person, an engineer in the United States who had been an activist during the days of the revolution said, "None of us were sad when we learned that Ahmad Khomeini had died."

Sons do much more than act as advisers to their fathers. If a marja' has many sons, the sons are likely to have various roles as well. Khomeini's son, Ahmad, for example, was referred to by one knowledgeable informant as being "apolitical" in the 1970s when his father was exiled to Iraq. The same informant describes Ahmad's older brother Mustafa, who died mysteriously shortly before the Revolution, as being the person who "ran his father's show." "Running the show", of course, involves, among other things, handling the money.

Sons and Money

One of the most controversial aspects of the marja'iya is the handling of the Imam's share of the khums—the sahm al-Imam. No one to whom I spoke ever accused a marja' of living lavishly or squandering the khums on themselves, though certainly historical sources have referred to this problem.[29] Their sons, on the other hand, are another question. For example, the suspicions about fiscal irresponsibility and irregularity abound in the case of the management of the khums by Ayatollah's al-Khu'i's sons. The 1970s the oil boom filled the coffers of the marja' to overflowing. Khums poured in from many places with large Shi'i populations, but particularly from the Gulf region. With Shirazi discredited there, the khums went to al-Khu'i. As mentioned above, al-Khu'i was renowned for living the way a marja' is traditionally supposed to live—in the most austere conditions. But while Ayatollah al-Khu'i was beyond question, his sons were not.

No one disputes that there have been financial irregularities. However, little is certain beyond this statement. It is hardly a task for me to sort out which rumors regarding possible financial mismanagement are true and which are not. What is of interest here is that such rumors abound, that they began before the death of Ayatollah al-Khu'i, and that they have persisted to this day.

As noted above, the 1970s saw a period of a huge increase in khums money flowing to al-Khu'i. It is alleged by some that by the 1980s the sum collected had been so great that other ulama were questioning the use of this money. Such accusations, say the detracors of the al-Khu'i family—led to al-Khu'i being compelled to begin a foundation that would be responsible for using the money for religiously sanctioned purposes: the building of mosques, hospitals, schools, orphanages, and the like. On the other hand, the al-Khu'i family claims that the foundation's establishment had nothing to do with pressure from the ulama or anyone else to properly utilize the funds. In fact, the al-Khu'is are quick to say that during the 1980s, during the Iran/Iraq war, it was nearly impossible to get khums from outside of Iraq. Al-Khu'i then issued a fatwa saying that the money should be utilized locally for religious purposes. This, then, according Majid al-Khu'i, was a very active time for building Shi'i institutions. He stated that in Pakistan alone there were 150 schools built and in India a hundred mosques. All of these were built before the Al-Khoei Foundation was established in northwest London.

If there are not out-and-out accusations of misuse of funds, then the problem of accountability still haunts the al-Khu'i family. With Ayatollah

[29] See, for example, Fischer, *Iran;* Nakash, *Shi'is,* p. 214.

al-Khu'i deceased, they are in an ambiguous position. The foundation is not the marja', yet there are still funds being utilized in the name of Ayatollah al-Khu'i. (The issue of the relationship between the foundation and a living marja' was discussed above.) On what basis is the foundation able to decide how the money is used? When the marja' is alive, he authorizes its use. On what authority do his relatives—the very informal leadership of the Foundation—decide the use of the money? For example, the decision to build the Al-Khoei Foundation Mosque in Queens was the decision of one of the sons of Ayatollah al-Khu'i, not of the local believers or of a marja'.

While there is criticism of such privilege and authority in the hands of the marja''s sons, there is, on the other hand, obvious respect as well. For example, Majid al-Khu'i was greatly in demand as a speaker at meetings. Shi'a flocked to his home on weekends and holidays to be in his presence. While part of this can be attributed to his own personal attributes, it must also be assumed that in large measure this is due to the fact that he is the son of the late marja' and, as such, reflects the charisma of his father. As Hanna Batatu has stated, "The descendents of 'ulama, even if they were not themselves 'ulama, always retained influence among the people and were respected through their families."[30] An Iraqi 'alim who now resides in London told a story about the escape of Ayatollah al-Hakim's sons, who was being pursued by the Iraqi government. An elderly woman, recognizing the marja''s son along the road, told him that she would fast until she was assured of his safety. This story was told in the context of a discussion about the sense of awe people feel in the presence of the marja'. It was quite obvious that he was suggesting that the charisma of the father also had the potential to be reflected in the son. Actually, al-Hakim's sons, most of whom have been killed by Saddam, were renowned for their role in building their father's marja'iya. Al-Hakim was revered by the Iraqi tribes since he, reputedly, was the first marja' in Najaf to care about them. Among other things, he sent his own sons out to their villages, and, when the tribesmen came to Najaf, his sons welcomed them warmly. According to one Iraqi, this behavior "touched the tribesmen's hearts. This is why his children are so respected and revered." It is significant for this discussion that, when this person spoke of al-Hakim's sons, he did not really differentiate between the actions of the sons and of al-Hakim himself. After praising al-Hakim's sons, he add-

30 Batatu, Hanna, The Old Social Classes and the Revolutionary Movements of Iraq: A Study of Iraq's Old Landed and Commercial Classes and of Its Communists, Ba'thists, and Free Officers (Princeton: Princeton University Press, 1978), p. 1141.

ed, "All the maraji' who preceded al-Hakim were Iranians and did not care about the welfare of Iraqi tribes. The name 'Muhsin'," he added, "means generous, and for those tribesmen he was such. They thought it was his title [not his name]. When I was a child, I thought al-Hakim was his title, since it means 'the wise man.'" Often when people speak about the marja', they don't talk about him as an individual but, rather, in a collective sense, meaning that the sons and those close to the marja' are all included.

As mentioned above, the son will likely be an 'alim, but it is not necessarily his purely religious or scholarly knowledge and duties that make him so essential to the marja'iya. In fact, even his activities of managing funds, running the marja''s offices, dealing with problems, and advising his father are all secondary. His most critical job is spreading his father's reputation in the first place. If that does not successfully occur, there will be no money to manage, no offices to administer, no substantial number of visitors to deal with. The statement sometimes heard from those close to the ulama establishment is that "the marja'iya is in the hands of the sons" is not that great an exaggeration, though there is certainly more to it than that. However, a son who has excellent interpersonal skills, is socially and politically astute, and is highly motivated and ambitious is key to the successful establishment of his father's renown as a marja'.

Obviously, there is a circular relationship here. The son, in his interactions with the community, attracts followers for his father. As more people become muqallid to his father, the son in turn gains prestige. The son who travels, meets with people easily, is eloquent, refined in his manners, and of sharp wit and intellect is the sort of person who is going to draw people to his father's marja'iya. As the list of those muqallid to his father grows, so does the esteem with which he is held.

Sons-in-law often serve in the same role as sons. Since the marja' always emerges from Middle Eastern patrilineal societies, this role might not seem an obvious one. However, one need only look at the marriage patterns of the ulama to see why sons-in-law would be such active players in the marja'iya. As Michael Fischer observed, "the elite do tend to intermarry and to recruit new talent to their marriage alliances as well as their work." [31] They tend to be related by blood or by marriage, and a newcomer to the circle will attempt to marry within it. As one informant said, "The talaba (students) always look for daughters of prominent ulama to get married to. It is the hawza culture." By marrying into an aspiring marja''s family, the talib would expect to serve as a representative for his father-in-law, who, of course, may already be a close relation. The

[31] Fischer, *Iran*, p. 89.

following example gives some idea of these complicated relationships. Ayatollah M. had at least one son A and one daughter. The daughter married Sayyid Q, an 'alim from the same town. The son A of Ayatollah M had a son who became a prominent 'alim. His daughter, in turn, married the son of Sayyid Q by Ayatollah M's daughter. Sayyid Q had other sons as well who married daughters of prominent ulama. In fact, this family is related to every major religious family in Iraq and Iran. The marriage alliance figure given by Fischer shows how the connections among the ulamsa extend from Iran to Iraq to Lebanon.[32]

The same sort of reciprocal relationship develops between the father-in-law and son-in-law as between the father and son. The son-in-law can advance his father-in-law's quest for the marja'iya and, in turn, benefit from the resources and prestige of the position.

The sons and sons-in-law, of course, cannot be the only people responsible for the spread of the reputation of the marja'. His students are also critical to the establishment of the marja'iya. Generally, the first thing one will learn from an 'alim is whom he studied with. If a madrasa-trained scholar says that he studied with Ayatollah al-Khu'i, one would automatically know certain things. The most basic would be that he studied in Najaf and had had a "rationalist" education. Najaf would not be the place to study 'irfan (mysticism) or even Islamic philosophy, but rather logic, fiqh, usul al-fiqh, Arabic grammar, and the like. If he completed his studies with Ayatollah al-Khu'i, he would be considered to have been thoroughly educated in the Islamic sciences of fiqh and usul al-fiqh (Islamic law and principle of jurisprudence). It would not have been necessary for a student to seek out another teacher. An 'alim's reputation is determined by who his teacher was. Conversely, the teacher's reputation is in good part the result of how many students he has. Having students costs money, as the teacher pays each student a living allowance. Consequently, the more khums a mujtahid receives, the more students he can afford. He is in need of students to spread his reputation so that people will pay khums to him.

Of course, not everyone who attended al-Khu'i's lectures was considered highly learned. Many were "back benchers." Therefore, the person who has completed his studies needs to receive an ijaza (a certificate) from his mentor as documentation. This system is comparable to the medieval university system in Europe at the point when an organized system of scholars and students was taking hold.[33] Nor does it seem

---

32 Fischer, *Iran,* p. 92

33 Charles Homer Haskins, *The Rise of Universities* (Cornell: Cornell University press, 1957).

unique to Shi'i madrasas. Speaking of madrasas in Sunni medieval Damascus, Chamberlain writes that "young people did not come to the city to enroll in specific madrasas for specific purposes, but rather sought advice concerning the teachers with whom they should study."[34]

The student generally feels a strong bond of loyalty to his teacher. As long as that teacher is alive, the student, no matter how promising, expects to live under his shadow. If the teacher is a marja' taqlid, as was al-Khu'i, then any one of his students with aspirations to the marja'iya would have been expected to wait until his demise before making a move to declare his own marja'iya. Instead, he would be expected to support his teacher's marja'iya. He should take satisfaction in knowing that any reputation of his own for excellence will enhance even more the reputation of the teacher under whose shadow he is happily basking. If he does see himself as a future candidate for the marja'iya, it will behoove him to spend his days writing, teaching, and, not least of all, aging.

But there are others, aside from sons and students, who may act as "hands" for the marja'iya. This is, after all, an international institution. The marja' is the spiritual guide for Shi'a around the world and relatively large numbers of wakils (representatives) are required. So, wherever there are Shi'a, there should be representatives of the marja'. Frequently, these are ulama who serve as imams of mosques. They lead prayers, give sermons, and counsel men and women on personal, spiritual, and social matters. As they perform these duties, they are in an excellent position to influence the believers regarding the choice of the marja'. Alternatively, they can be travelling preachers who perform the rawda (the ritual services commemorating the death of Imam Husayn) or give speeches. However, the fact that they are representatives of the marja' does not automatically mean that they will try to influence people to follow that marja'. After all, unless they are mujtahids themselves, they are not officially qualified to judge the marja' for others, even if they themselves have consulted with mujtahids who are 'adil and muhtat. In cases where they are called upon to give guidance about whom to follow, the representatives might tell the seeker that there are a few people eligible to be a marja' and tell him or her about the qualifications and characteristics of each.

A cleric who acts as a representative for the marja' is generally given an ijaza, a certificate, that, depending on the type of ijaza a person has, permits him to assume certain responsibilities. The highest-level ijaza states that a cleric is qualified to answer a petitioner's questions based on

---

[34] Michael Chamberlain, *Knowledge and Social Practice In Medieval Damascus, 1190-1350* (Cambridge: Cambridge University Press, 1994), p. 87.

the cleric's understanding of the marja''s overall rulings and opinions. The answer should be in keeping with the general philosophy of the marja', but the marja' does not have to be consulted on that particular issue. More commonly, a cleric is given an ijaza that allows him simply to give an answer to the petitioner that has already been provided by the marja' in response to other cases presented before the marja'. In such a case, the cleric refers to the marja''s risala and other writings for a specific answer. No judgment on the part of the cleric is required. In either case, one of the primary duties of the representative is to collect the khums. He forwards a portion of it to the marja' and is authorized to keep some of it for local use and as his own means of support. Naturally, the paying of khums would be a regular topic for sermons.

Sometimes the representative is not a cleric. In the Gulf region, for example, the representatives sometimes are businessmen. In such cases, their only role is to collect the khums, all of which is either sent to the marja' or, if the marja' authorizes it, used for local religious or charitable purposes. The businessman would not be expected to demand payment for his services. Why, then, would he wish to act as a representative? The answer is actually simple. He draws business to himself by being associated with the prestigious name and sanctity of the marja'. He would be more likely to be seen as a pious, honest person himself and one worthy to do business with. He, of course, would also be paying the religious tax on his own income.

Why does the khums have to go to the marja' at all? Why can't it just be used locally? As mentioned above, sometimes the marja' does permit communities to keep the khums for local use,, as did al-Khu'i during the Iran/Iraq war. The more likely scenario, however, is for the marja' to permit a community to keep a proportion of the khums for its local use and to send the remainder to him. With the khums, then, the marja' is able to support projects throughout the world and to take care of the humanitarian needs of Shi'a who are affected by wars, natural disasters, or other hardships. While this system allows for broader, more even distribution of funds, it spreads the marja''s prestige. The funding for projects comes associated with the marja''s name, thereby enhancing his reputation.

But why does the businessman in the Gulf need to give his money to the marja'? Wouldn't his own reputation be better served by making local contributions to charity in his own name? If he built a recreation center for the youth of his community, for example, and had it named after himself, wouldn't this advance his own standing and guarantee that he would have control over the finances? For a devout Shi'ite, one answer to this question is obvious: the funds are purified when presented to the

Imam through the representation of the marja'. Should funds be at all tainted—for example, by having been obtained in a manner not sanctioned by religion, such as by the sale of alcohol—paying khums relieves the burden of any misdeed committed.

There is another aspect to this issue, as well—the long-standing relationship between ulama and merchants. Ahmad Ashraf (1988) has clearly elucidated this relationship:

> Merchants and commercial trade are esteemed in Islamic civilization. The society of Mecca, the birthplace of Islam, was already a major center of local, regional and, at times, international trade. The city of Mecca itself was, at the time of the rise of Islam, dominated by the merchant patricians. . . Friday congregational prayer, one of the most important Islamic institutions articulating the religious community and the state, coincided with the day on which the business activities of the weekly bazaar heightened because the people of the town and surrounding areas gathered in the marketplace for business transactions. . . The prophet Muhammad, whose first wife as well as many members of his own clan were among the city's prosperous merchants, himself engaged in trade on behalf of his wife.

Any religious reform of the world thus included the reform of the bazaar because it was the main arena of extra-familial sociability and the main public center of the community of believers. Religious and commercial images were projected by Islamic ideas onto the preferred norms for religious community.[35]

It should not be surprising, therefore, to find such close links between the ulama and the businessmen in the Gulf region and elsewhere. These relationships seem to be merely a modern extension of very old ties.

The Selection of Wakils and Representatives

While a marja' must be content with the sons given to him, he can be more selective of his sons-in-law. Of course, there would be a limited range of eligible young men to choose from. Issues of kinship and personal relationships narrow the field considerably. As we have seen in the case cited above, cousin marriage, marriage between the offspring of close friends, marriages that will strengthen the relationships among ulama—these are all highly valued among clerical families.

What about the other wakils? How are they selected? Again, personal relationships play a major role. The centrality of wasta, connections, to Middle Eastern life is well known. Without wasta one often finds it hard

---

[35] Ahmad Ashraf, "Bazaar-Mosque Alliance: The Social Basis of Revolts and Revolutions," *Politics, Culture, and Society* 1 (1988), p. 539–40.

to obtain suitable employment, get into a university, or collect a package from the post office. Wasta is as central to the marja'iya as it is to all other aspects of Middle Eastern life. It is always assumed that a person who serves as a representative is well connected either to the marja' himself or to those around him. No one questions the wasta system.

The marja'-wakil relationship is definitely a reciprocal and often a highly personal one. It is not just a matter of the marja' rewarding the son of a loyal friend or contributor by sending him off on a job. Indeed, the wakil becomes a player in the entire process of the marja'iya. The marja''s wakils, who may also be linked to him through marriage, serve as his hands in reaching out to the Shi'a throughout the world. When ties and feelings of loyalty are very strong, wakils might put forward "their" mujtahid as a marja'. Such cases are always portrayed in the same manner: "Ayatollah (or Sayyid) X is (was) so learned that his followers came to him and begged him to write a risala to announce his marja'iya." Depending on the circumstances (which will be discussed more fully in chapter four), the mujtahid may or may not choose to write a risala or its equivalent. If he does, then his close associates can then go about trying to spread the word of his marja'iya.

Under such circumstances, it is, therefore, understandable how a number of people can come forward as maraji' simultaneously, and why there is such a person who is referred to as a "local" marja'. The Shirazis of Karbala provide a case in point. During Mahdi Shirazi's lifetime the people most likely to follow him were themselves either residing in Karbala or had close links to that city.

Why would have Ayatollah Mahdi Shirazi remained a "local" marja' and not have been more widely recognized? Part of the answer to this question lies with his wakils, for they have as much to do with selecting the marja' as the marja' does with selecting his wakils. This is not peculiar to Shirazi; it is the situation for all maraji'.

Sayyid Muhammad Bahraloom now resides in London but had been very closely associated with the late Ayatollah al-Hakim. He spoke about how his students at the hawza (as well as his sons) would leave the hawza to do tabligh (missionary work) among the tribal people on Thursdays and Fridays. According to Bahraloom, "During the months of Ramadan, Muharram, and Safar the students would go throughout Iraq, and the students would practice their knowledge. What distinguished al-Hakim's leadership was that he used to send representatives to 95% of the cities in Iraq. This was not intitiated by al-Hakim himself, but he did encourage it more than his predecessors." Such teaching efforts were not limited to Iraq. Students who came from other countries would return during the summer months to their homes and be expected to give sermons. Praise of their great teacher, al-Hakim, would be part and parcel of such sermons. Thus, the more students a mujtahid has, the more his name will spread. Again, this is a reciprocal relationship. The mujtahid has to draw students. He can do this by paying for a student to study at the hawza and by developing a reputation for being knowledgeable. The student, by representing the marja' outside the hawza, spreads the reputation of the marja', encourages the contribution of khums to the marja', and allows the marja' to support more students.

However, this is only one type of representation. There are people who are specifically designated as official representatives of the marja'. These are people who have more or less established positions and are held in some esteem in their communities, often men with a reputation for leadership or scholarship of their own. The process by which such individuals become representatives is very interesting. When, for example, Ayatollah al-Khu'i died, potential representatives throughout the world watched carefully the various mujtahids coming forward as maraji'. After the death of a grand marja' such as al-Khu'i, there are always several possible candidates. Some representatives will, of course, back a particular person immediately. Others will wait to see who is gaining the lead in terms of popularity.

Timing is very important here. If a prospective representative acts too hastily, he might set himself up as the representative of the "failed" candidate, a person who lacks broad appeal. No matter how effective he might be in promoting his candidate, if others throughout the world are not effective in the same way, then he will find himself having backed someone who has little prestige or wealth (i.e., khums) to utilize to further establish his position. On the other hand, by waiting too long, he risks being upstaged by another representative. There should not be overlap in representation. A representative has a designated location or population for which he is responsible. Representatives should not be competing with one another. This would sow confusion as to whom to pay khums to and could also breed contention as factions form around different representatives.

As for the other part of the equation, it is equally important that the marja' select representatives who are going to perform well in their job. This person's character and reputation must not be in question as he is a reflection of the marja'iya on the local level. Yet, beyond these general traits, there is much room for disagreement as to the type of person who makes the ideal representative. He must appeal to the rank and file, who in turn must trust him with their money. Still, the Shi'i community is extremely diverse. It is divided along ethnic, national, and ideological lines. While some wakils may be dealing with a more or less homogeneous population, many are not. Somehow, the wakils facing various groups and factions must gain the trust of a wide spectrum of individuals to do their jobs.

A relative of Ayatollah al-Khu'i said that in Iran, the marja' had two representatives. One had a reputation for being "tight." He was respected for this as it is considered admirable to be cautious with the "Imam's money." The other wakil was reputed to be lavish in his expenditures and did not live as austerely as some thought he should, yet the latter was a good manager and invested the khums in business ventures that provided the funds for the al-Khu'i School in Mashhad. Such expenditures attract even more khums. Which of the two was the better wakil is open to dispute.

Representing More Than One Marja'

Some wakils have fairly well defined roles. They have an ijaza for one marja' and are seen as the official spokesperson, at least at some level, for that marja'. Shaykh Fadhil Sahlani at the Al-Khoei Foundation in Queens, New York, was the official representative of the late grand ayatollah in North America, for example. There are other ulama or individuals connected with the marja'iya who act as liaisons for more than one marja'. They do not tell a person to whom he should be muqallid; they simply explain the major ideas of the maraji', pointing out significant tendencies that may differentiate them from one another. Whether or not a person will be a sole representative or not is decided by a multitude of factors, the benefits to the wakil being one of them.

If one is a wakil for a well-recognized marja', then a good deal of prestige and stability can come from representing that one marja'. However, one will have to be very much the "company man" to remain in that position. Keeping in mind that the marja'iya is not a one-man show but is an intricate network of relatives and representatives, it may or may not fit someone's style to be this closely linked to a single marja'. Needless to say, if a mujtahid does not have a significant number of muqallids in the area to which the wakil is assigned, then the benefits to the wakil can be negligible. The wakil will not be receiving khums and will probably not be sought out to give lectures or receive dignataries. Another person may see it as beneficial to represent several maraji' in a looser, non-official way. He would still have access to the maraji' to answer questions but would not be a spokesman for any of them. This is a riskier approach because he would not be as visible in his role as a wakil for any given marja' and people might turn to the official wakil to pay khums. However, this individual would have more freedom and not be so directly under the control of anyone.

There is a more ambiguous position that a wakil may assume. He may himself be a supporter of a particular mujtahid but may find it imprudent to be too vocal about representing him. Earlier we spoke about the Mudarrisi brothers being representatives for Ayatollah Shirazi in the Gulf. It is interesting to note that Joseph Kostiner cites Hadi Mudarrisi as being Khomeini's representative.[36] There is no reason to believe that either claim is incorrect. Shirazi would not have wished to appear to be putting himself on a par with Khomeini. (Indeed, in later years, when Shirazi had a falling out with Khomeini, the person who acted as the intermediary between the two was careful to refer to Shirazi, in Khomeini's presence, as "Sayyid" Shirazi, not "Ayatollah.") Khomeini's success relied upon being seen as the ultimate Shi'i leader. While the Mudarrisis may have been paving the way for the future marja'iya of Shirazi, they would not necessarily have been very open about this. Their foremost objective would have been, as Kostiner points out, to foment revolution in the Gulf. This was most likely to have been accomplished under the banner of Khomeini.

Wasta and the Marja'iya

In their book, *Wasta: The Hidden Force in Middle Eastern Society*, Cunningham and Sarayrah provide the following definition.

> *Wasata,* or *wasta,* means the middle, and is assoicated with the verb *yatawassat,* to steer conflicting parties toward a middle point, or compromise. *Wasta* refers to both the act and the person who mediates or intercedes. . . An individual or a *wasta* delegation of elders *(jaha)* may mediate or intereced on behalf of a young woman or man for marriage, or build a coalition on any issue, or assist in resolving conflict. The *wasta* seeks to achieve that which is asumed to be otherwise unattainable by the supplicant.[37]

Just as kinship is central to the structure and organization of Middle Eastern life, so too is *wasta*. People speak as though nothing could be accomplished without it. One "must have" a wasta to get a job or a promotion, to facilitate getting a government permit, to gain admittance to a university, and, perhaps, to even pass a university course. It is simply a fact of life. The running of the marja'iya is no exception. In order to become a representative, one needs links to the marja'iya. Kinship and

---

[36] Joseph Kostiner, "Kuwait and Bahrain," in Shireen Hunter, *The Politics of Islamic Revivalism: Diversity and Unity* (Bloomington: Indiana University Press, 1988), p. 121.

[37] Robert Cunningham and Yasin K. Sarayrah, *Wasta: The Hidden Force In Middle Eastern Society* (Westport, Conn.: Praeger, 1993), p. 1.

connections are the most important qualifications. Of course, if one is connected either through kinship or friendships, one's qualities are known. However, it is generally recognized that these connections will override other issues.

What is also interesting in terms of wasta is the manner in which governments interact with the marja'iya. The government is quite capable of enhancing the marja'iya of one person over another by dealing with the representatives of the favored marja'. For example, in the town of Samarra, there were representatives of two maraji', Ayatollahs al-Khu'i and al-Sadr (who will be discussed in Chapter 5). The government dealt only with al-Khu'i's representative.

And the government, prior to the crackdown on the Shi'a, was eager to do favors for the representatives. One informant said that his father, who was a prosperous businessman, often needed to have paperwork expedited. Being muqallid to al-Khu'i, he turned to al-Khu'i's representative for help in getting the necessary permissions. The government agency in being responsive to the requests of the representative gained legitimacy in the eyes of the people by appearing to be respectful and helpful to a religious leader.

Institution Building

The following is excerpted from a booklet entitled *Al-Khoei Foundation, Concept and Projects, 1992:*

> Shia communities voluntarily fund projects worldwide, through a network of marja'iya representatives. Normally they are authorized to collect donations and religious contributions from the community and liaise between the marja'iya and the community on projects' allocations.
>
> Shia communities throughout the world also play a fundamental role in selecting the spiritual leader of the community who holds the position of marja'iya and who is normally given the title Grand Ayatollah, where he emerges by consensus as the most outstanding person in religious knowledge. The grand Ayatullah's emergence is a grassroots process where theological institutions and schools play an important intermediary role in identifying and endorsing the position of the ran ayatullah to hold the position of marja'iya on behalf of their constitutents. Although the Shi'a communities are the main beneficiaries of the marja'iya projects, the access and benefits of its projects are not limited only to Shias. . .

The booklet enumerates the kinds of projects undertaken by the Foundation, stating that "its social role is most visible in areas of need and at times of crisis." They cite projects in India such as building schools, drilling water wells, and providing water for villages. The Al-Khoei Foundation played a prominent role in establishing orphanages and aiding victims in the Lebanese civil war. During the Iran-Iraq War, it "undertook to re-house more than 2000 Iraqi families from the Basra district who lost their homes during the bombardment of their city."

The collection and distribution of khums is central to the marja'iya. The payment of khums is the most obvious way for the devout Shi'ite to express his taqlid to a marja'. The building of mosques or setting up of humanitarian projects is the most obvious way for the marja' to express his status to the community. This circulation of funds is a means to bind together a social order with the high-ranking ulama at the top. The establishment of the Al-Khoei Foundation was the most visible expression of this link between the marja' and the people. Its establishment was made possible—indeed, some say obligatory—with the khums resulting from the phenomenal oil revenues of the 1970s. While other sources of income have provided funding for marja' in the past—the Oudh bequest, funds from the Shi'i Indian state of Awadh (Oudh) that involved a loan to a British governor in 1825 from the King of Oudh, the interest of which was to be paid to mujtahids in Najaf and Karbala to be distributed to needy person[38]; the corpse traffic, the khums paid loyally over the years by peasants, tribesmen, businessmen, etc.—nothing could rival the amount of religious tax generated by oil wealth.

But just how does khums get distributed? The marja'iya does not operate like a government agency. While the Khoei Foundation as it exists today in London is more or less recognizable as a Western-style foundation, it came into existence in its current form only in the late 1980s. Many of its projects were either established or underway before then. How did they come about? Was there a grand building plan? Was there a budget for various categories of community needs? The answer to these questions is best expressed in the words of an informant who said, "The ulama's actions are, by and large, accidental: no planning, no long-term outlook. All that you hear about the ulama from Western analysts [i.e., their organization and coordinated efforts towards fulfilling goals] is far from the truth."

What does seem to determine what gets done is the ambition, the energy, and the persuasiveness of the wakil. The successful wakil will generate enthusiasm for a project, such as building a school, in his local community. Such enthusiasm can be demonstrated by increased contributions of khums, especially when an increased number of people begin to pay their religious taxes. The backing he has from the community will allow him to approach the marja' with a strong case for financial support

[38] Juan R. I. Cole, "'Indian Money' and the Shi'i Shrine Cities of Iraq, 1786–1850," *Middle Eastern Studies* 22/4 (1986), pp. 461–80; Nakash, *Shi'is,* pp. 249–53.

for the project. It behooves the marja' to keep his representatives happy; yet because he will have many representatives scattered throughout the world, he must balance pleasing one wakil with the needs of maintaining good relations with all his other wakils. It goes without saying that the wakil's prestige in the eyes of the community will be enhanced if he receives financial backing from the marja' for proposed projects.

Competition among wakils—even ones who might live on opposite sides of the world—can be intense. One 'alim, trying to build an Islamic school in North America went to a marja' for funds that he had been expecting to receive for this purpose. However, another wakil visited the marja' in question and was able to persuade him that the needs of his community in a totally different part of the world superseded those of his North American counterpart.

Before a mosque, hospital, or other social institution is founded, the local community would have to cooperate in negotiating for land, building licenses, contracts, etc. In other words, the local community would have to express its desire to have an institution built by a marja'. It might seem obvious that a local community would only be too happy to receive the funds for a mosque or a school or some other institution from a marja' taqlid. However, this is not necessarily the case. A community might reject the funds for such a project for a variety of reasons. First, it may be that the Shi'a in the area are not in agreement over the selection of the marja'. In fact, the issue might be a very divisive one in a community struggling for some semblance of unity. Those who do not make taqlid to the marja' offering the support may feel that their own marja' would lose prestige by such an endeavor. In cases where temporal politics are also involved, the situation is far more sensitive, as it was during the lifetimes of al-Khu'i and Khomeini. Other communities may simply feel that they do not want "outside" control of a local insitution. In the United States this has been an issue where Shi'i community leaders have been raised as Americans. This more assimilated population tends to see religious organization as a local matter. They also tend not to have such strong links to the marja'iya as those who reside in traditional Shi'i societies or who are latecomers to the United States [39] (The issue of the marja'iya and the West will be discussed in chapter eight.)

[39] Linda Walbridge, *Without Forgetting the Imam: Lebanese Shi'ism in an American Community* (Detroit: Wayne State University Press, 1997), pp. 71–75.

The Infallible Marja'?

Of hereditary saints in the Middle East, Ernest Gellner wrote,

> He who is treated as a saint becomes one. The respect he is shown enables him to arbitrate effectively and thereby display and prove his sanctity. The donations he receives enable him to entertain generously without seeming to count the cost and thereby, one again, to demonstrate his saintly status.[40]

While the hereditary saint belongs to a different realm than the scholarly theologian, the realm of folk Islam, the same principles apply. The marja' is a marja' because he is recognized as one and because people pay khums to him. His expenditure of the khums enhances his reputation and increases his influence as a jurist. Just how great is this influence? This is a question that will be answered throughout the rest of this book, but a few comments are in order now. One of the questions that I explored throughout my research was whether people viewed their marja' as infallible. After all, he is the representative of the Twelfth Imam, who was considered infallible himself. The answers to this question are intriguing and, once again, shed light on the very nature of the institution.

One highly educated person responded that "kinship, education and religion all become intertwined, and, as a result, you get the aura of infallibility" with the marja'. He said that "those who are connected with the highest-level ulama, whether they be ulama themselves or married into ulama families or have a lot of contact with them,are the most likely to have the greatest reverence for the ulama. People outside that circle are less likely to see grand ayatollahs as infallible." The father of this individual was wealthy and paid a considerable amount of khums to his marja', for which he received great deal of clerical respect. He apparently saw the marja''s rulings as infallible. Contrast this with the comments of an 'alim who resides in the United States: "I know them all," he said, referring to the major mujtahids considered maraji' today. I am linked to them all through marriage. So I know that they are not infallible."

Thus, it appears to be those who are in a middling position—not so far from the center that they have virtually no contact with the marja'iya, nor so close that they have easy access to him and his family—who see the marja' as infallible. This makes for great variation in attitudes towards the marja'.

---

[40] Ernest Gellner, "Tribalism and the State in the Middle East," in Philip S. Khoury and Joseph Kostiner, *Tribes and State Formation In the Middle East* (Berkeley: University of California Press, 1990), p. 118.

Chapter Four

The Selling of the Iranian Marja'iya

SHI'ISM AND IRAN ARE SO CLOSELY identified with one another that there is a tendency to see the two as being inseparably linked. Certainly Iranians identify themselves as being "the Shi'a" to the exclusion of all other nationalities. In conversations about religion, they often have to be reminded that there are Arab, Pakistani, Indian, and other Shi'a. Ulama-dominated Shi'ism has been the official religion of Iran since Safavid times, and as Lapidus writes, "The Safavids. . . eliminated Sunni 'ulama' and Sufi holy men, and made the Shi'i 'ulama' the sole representatives of Islam in Iran."[41] On the other hand, Sunnis have always been the politically dominant religious community in what we know today as Iraq. While the Shi'i divines may have, as Batatu says, "occupied a position of no little importance,"[42] they have never occupied a central position in the state such as the ulama of Iran have. This, in spite of the fact that Iraq is home to the holiest of the shrine cities.

It was also Iran, through its successful revolution, which brought the world's attention to the Shi'i ulama and to the institution of the marja'iya. There has been a plethora of books and articles written about the Islamic Revolution, the government of the Islamic Republic of Iran, and the role of the Iranian Shi'ite clergy in overturning the monarchy and running the new government. Yet it has become apparent that, while Iran created renewed interest in the marja'iya, it has failed to sustain and

---

41 Ira M. Lapidus, "Tribes and State Formation in the Middle East," in Philip S. Khoury and Joseph Kostiner, *Tribes and State Formation In the Middle East* (Berkeley: University of California Press, 1990), p. 38.

42 Batatu, *Old Social Classes*, p. 44.

uphold the very elements of the institution that have infused it with meaning for the believers. This failure is due partially to modern Iranian governmental policies and intervention in matters that have traditionally been outside of government control. It is also due to the actions of the "ultimate marja'" himself, Khomeini. In this chapter we will explore Khomeini's role in the marja'iya. Ultimately, we will attempt to show how the histories and modern politics of both Iran and Iraq have, in rather curious ways, have shifted the center of Shi'ism from Iran to Iraq—or, more accurately, caused religious leadership to be more defused but with its focal point being Najaf.

Yet, it is not easy to separate religious affairs into categories of Iranian and Iraqi (or Arab). Perhaps one of the most perplexing issues in sorting out the workings of the higher-ranking Shi'i ulama is nationality. Repeatedly the ulama and the laymen with whom I spoke would state that, when it comes to the ulama, nationality does not matter. This statement would appear to make a great deal of sense since the ulama are so thoroughly intermarried, especially between Iraqis and Iranians. Furthermore, their lives tend to revolve around religious education in theological universities that have the same traditions regardless of whether they are in Iran or Iraq. Up until the founding of the hawza in Qom, Najaf was far and away the most important Shi'i university, and ulama, regardless of nationality, studied there. Indeed, Ayatollah al-Khu'i himself, though so closely identified with Iraq, was from Iran.

Why is it, then, that when one does dig more deeply, nationality begins to surface as a very sensitive problem? It might be argued that any tensions found are actually the result of Iraqi and Iranian government policies and rivalries and interference by foreign powers. Certainly, these were factors in the founding of the hawza of Qom in the early 1920s, as it was then that the revolt against the British in Iraq was going on. The Shi'i ulama had been deeply involved in the affair and even sought assistance from the Persian government. When the revolt failed, the threat of arrest drove many of them to flee to Iran.[43] By then other ulama had begun to gather in Qom from various parts of Iran to revive the madrasa system begun in the early Safavid period. The seminaries had prospered in Qom, as people were drawn to the holy shrine of the eighth Imam's sister, Fatima, but these schools had petered out by the early part of the nineteenth century. The ulama found to their dismay that Reza Shah was no more hospitable than Iraq's British backed monarchy. Some were able to return to Iraq with the proviso that they sign an agreement stating

[43] Phoebe Marr, *The Modern History of Iraq* (Boulder, Colo.: Westview, 1985), pp. 32–34, and Battatu, *Old Social Classes*, pp. 1141–47.

that they would not become involved in Iraqi politics.

Traffic had been going the other way for centuries. Juan Cole writes,

> The political turmoil of eighteenth-century Iran, with its Afghan invasions and the fall of the Safavids, also encouraged large numbers of Iranian refugees to settle in Najaf and Karbala. In the nineteenth century Iranian merchants and noblemen resided there out of a pious wish to be near the shrines or because Iran turned politically dangerous for them. Although Iranian immigrants over time assimilated to Iraq, many maintained their distinctive national costume, knowledge of Persian and underground allegiance to Iran. Because of its prevailing Shi'ism and the large Iranian ethnic element, Ottoman officials saw Karbala as a potential fifth column.[44]

Certainly, the hostile relations existing between Iran and Iraq through most of this century have not served to promote good relations.

The role of politics in defining the line between Iran and Iraq cannot be overemphasized. In spite of that, there are obviously deep ethnic issues that need to to be explored. Nakash, for example, refers to Indian money in the eighteenth and nineteenth centuries going to Persian rather than Arab mujtahids because the ulama in India felt more of an affinity for the Persians.[45] Today, Arab Shi'a will commonly say, with some resentment, that the marja'iya was in the hands of Iranians until al-Hakim became the marja'—i.e., long before the Pahlavis, Arab nationalists, or Ba'thists were around. Batatu has written that

> at least in the past it was possible to sense in Najaf itself an undercurrent of tension between Iranian and Arab ulama not dissimilar to that which prevailed between the Greek and Arab clergy within the Orthodox church in Syria and Palestine. Some of the Iranian men of religion tended to look down on their Iraqi counterparts and entertained the notion that Iranians were, on the whole, more devoted to their faith than the Arabs and that had the religious message not descneded upon an Arab prophet, no Arab would have embraced Islam. At any rate, Iraq's Shi'is are clearly more comfortable with their own kind and prefer that rela leadership should be in the hands of Shi'is who are Iraqi.[46]

Rivalries between Najaf and Karbala have a great deal to do with the fact that there is such a strong Persian influence in Karbala. Oddly enough, some of the very people who speak in disparaging terms about the Iranian domination of Karbala trace at least part of their recent ancestry to Iran. This includes people from various Iraqi cities.

---

[44] Juan R. I. Cole, "Mafia, Mob and Shiism in Iraq: The Rebellion of Ottoman Karbala," *Past and Present* 112 (1986), p. 115.

[45] Nakhash, *Shi'is,* p. 211.

[46] Batatu, "Shi'i Organizations," p. 199.

Searching for the basis of ethnic identity among Shi'a is not the purpose of this book. The fact that ethnic rivalries exist explains some of the dynamics of the modern marja'iya. On the other hand, there are also circumstances that diminish these ethnic differences. For example, according to Majid Khui, the Iran-Iraq War was a time when such differences become less consequential:

> The war was very difficult for us. We had to help both sides financially—Iran and Iraq. One city like Basra was being bombarded by the Iranian side, so people went to Najaf and they needed food and clothes from us [the al-Khui administrative offices]. Our offices in Iran were doing the same thing for the Iranians. When the Iraqis bombed a place in Iran, people would go to Tehran or Qom and my father's offices would have to do something for them. They are all Shi'ites. It doesn't matter if they are Iranian or Iraq. The Iranian government wanted some clear fatwa to support them, and the Iraqi government wanted a fatwa to support them. It was very difficult to balance this.

While issues of ethnic identity are murky, at least among ulama families, the historical processes affecting the marja'iya are a bit clearer.

Iran's Marja'iya

In 1945 Ayatollah Husayn Tabataba'i Borujerdi began teaching in Qom, thereby increasing Qom's prestige until it rivaled that of Najaf.[47] Like al-Hakim and the ulama who prevailed at Najaf, Borujerdi was of the "rationalist" school, holding usul al-fiqh (jurisprudence) as the most highly esteemed discipline. Philosophy, mysticism, and 'irfan, subjects of deep concern to mujtahids such as Ruhallah Musawi Khomeini and 'Allamah Sayyid Muhammad Husayn Tabataba'i, were anathema to Borujerdi and indeed to the majority of Usuli ulama.

Borujerdi was clearly recognized as being highly learned in the Islamic sciences. However, for all his prestige and his designation as "sole marja'," (at least by historians focusing on Iran), until his death in 1960, his legacy is that he was apolitical. As Abrahamian writes

> Borujerdi was the epitome of the archconservative cleric who bolstered the status quo while claiming to keep out of politics. In the words of one religious dissident, these conservative ayatollahs turned the clerical establishment into a pillar of the Pahlavi regime.[48]

Nonetheless, the ulama who became famous for their activism, including Ayatollah Khomeini, remained silent about their frustration over Bo-

---

[47] Moojan Momen, *An Introduction to Shi'i Islam* (Oxford: George Ronald, 1985), pp. 247–48.

[48] Abrahamian, *Khomeinism*, p. 8.

rujerdi's refusal to protest governmental policies, policies that tended to weaken the role of the ulama and that promoted secular, irreligious trends in society.

In fact, as Dabashi documents, Ayatollah Morteza Mutahhari who was so instrumental in developing the ideology of the revolution, actually praised Borujerdi as being progressive in some social issues.

> Such critical issues as having wide-ranging religious and social concerns (instead of being narrow-mindedly preoccupied with obscure juridical hypothesis), seeking to advance the cause of Islamic unification, (instead of being trapped in sectarian infighting), propagating Islam in 'the West' (instead of being propagated by Christian or, even worse, secular European ideologies), advancing the cause of modern education (instead of being branded as reactionary and anti-intellectual), and ultimately organizing the financial backbone of the clerical class (instead of wasting and mismanaging this great source of independence from governments) were all among the primary concerns of Mutahhari as a leading ideologue of the Islamic cause.[49]

The fact that Borujerdi was not openly criticized by those opposed to his policies reveals something very important about the marja'iya. Someone who has risen to be the undisputed marja' of the Shi'i world, or at least a large portion of it, has developed a network of relationships that cannot be easily unraveled by disagreement over policies. Khomeini's and Borujerdi's families were closely linked by marriage. The two men were known to be close friends. These personal relationships are often sufficient to override many significant differences. Also, that Borujerdi was so highly esteemed for his learning and widely recognized as the marja' taqlid al-azim of the Shi'a made him off limits to open criticism.

Regardless of personal loyalties and respect, activists such as Mutahhari and Khomeini were anxious that Borujerdi's successor not separate the marja'iya from politics and that the clergy take their role as leaders of society and of government. As a result of their activities, the Shah, who had supported Borujerdi, now began to support al-Hakim, who resided in Najaf and was an Iraqi citizen, as the grand marja' so as to weaken the marja'iya in Iran.

Because of the Iranian Revolution, scholarly attention has been focused during the past couple of decades on analyzing this phenomenon from a variety of political, social, cultural, theological, and historical perspectives. It is not my task to repeat all that has been said about Ayatollah Khomeini and his role in changing the course of Iranian society. Also, it should be clear that Khomeini was just one player in a worldwide Islamic revival. Even among Iranian Shi'a, he was just one of sever-

---

[49] Dabashi, *Theology*, p. 167.

al very active opponents of the Shah among the clergy. That the conditions for a full-fledged revolution based on religious ideology were ripe in Iran and not in other Islamic countries, such as Iraq, have been addressed elsewhere.

A few facts should be reiterated. First, in 1963 and 1964 Khomeini led protests against the Iranian government, resulting in his arrest and then his exile to Turkey, where he remained for eleven months. In October 1965 he went to Najaf, spending the next thirteen years refining his theory of Islamic government and preaching against the Pahlavi regime. Finally, he was forced to leave Iraq. His attempt to go to Kuwait was thwarted by the Kuwaiti government, which had begun to get a sense of Khomeini's ambitions, so he ultimately went to Paris to pursue his long-distance campaign against the Shah.

Khomeini's Influence

Authors such as Dabashi note that Khomeini was at an advantage by being exiled to Iraq because he was outside the control of the Iranian government. The Iraqi government, which had hostile relations with Iran, also saw fit not to interfere with him. In terms of his struggle against the Pahlavi regime, these were indeed advantages. However, in terms of promoting a more universal crusade, it seems not to have been so. Khomeini was "free" only to lambast the Iranian regime, but he was not free to criticize Iraq. He took advantage of access to Iraqi Persian broadcasting to beam his campaign against the Pahlavi monarchy. While Khomeini did send messages through his associates to the Ba'thists, criticizing them for their campaign against Shi'i activists in Iraq, his protests were low key. His most extreme measure was to publicly condemn the Iraqi government for executing three clerics and to cease his regular class in the hawza for a few days.[50]

Many Iraqi activists have noted Khomeini's relative silence in regard to Saddam's dictatorship and suppression of Shi'ism. While one might argue that Khomeini had no other choice but to focus only on Iran, this does not seem likely. For one thing, he was willing to risk imprisonment and worse when in Iran, so that it was not likely to be fear that motivated his silence towards Iraq. Also, when he went to Paris, he still continued to direct all of his efforts to overturning the Shah.

That Khomeini was not censored by the Iraqi government is significant. For all of Khomeini's rhetoric about a "universal" Islamic revolution, Khomeini addressed his writings and speeches to an Iranian

---

[50] Talib M. Aziz, "Islamic Political Theory," p. 50.

audience, avoiding open criticism of the Iraqi regime. Both the Iranian and Iraqi governments have tried to manipulate the marja'iya in much the same way that they have attempted to manipulate everyone and everything else. Each certainly wanted to promote a marja' who was friendly to its own government, and each has very actively attempted to stir up rivalries and antipathies among the senior ulama. Both the Iranian and Iraqi governments have long recognized the importance of the marja'iya. These governments know that the marja' can have a tremendous influence on the muqallid so that it is in their best interest to win or coerce the support of the marja.' The marja' can act as a mediator between the government and the people, or he can, as was the case with Khomeini and al-Sadr, be the leader of rebellion against the government. As Mallat states, when the Iraqi police were arresting Shi'i demonstrators, they were very interested in ascertaining to whom the demonstrators were muqallid.[51] Because of the differences among the marja', the answer to this question would speak volumes.

To mention only one example of government manipulation of the institution, a high-level bureaucrat from Baghdad came to Najaf while Khomeini resided there. The bureaucrat visited Khomeini before he visited al-Khu'i. This was an obvious affront to Ayatollah al-Khu'i, who far outranked Khomeini in rank among the ulama and who should have received the first visit. The official, when questioned, explained to Ayatollah al-Khu'i, "It would not matter if I visited you first or last. Everyone knows you are our grand marja'. I cannot diminish your status. Khomeini is our guest." A visit such as this would be highly visible, and the bureaucrat's violation of protocol would have been interpreted as a snub to al-Khu'i and sign of respect for Khomeini.

Realistically, Khomeini and al-Khu'i could not have been expected to be on cordial terms. Al-Khu'i's strict legalism was opposed to Khomeini's mystical rationalism, and their disagreement over the role of the jurist in government added to the usual rivalries found among mujtahids. It may seem logical that Khomeini would have won over many sympathizers in Najaf. After all, he was the model of the religious figure fighting tyranny. He should have been an attractive figure to the Iraqis who have experienced a good deal of tyranny in their country. He would have been expected to be an appealing alternative to the apolitical, non-activist al-Khu'i, who did not offer any remedy in the temporal sphere for the suffering of the Iraqi Shi'a. This was not the case. Khomeini did not win over the followers of al-Khu'i essentially for two reasons. First, al-Khu'i had been teaching in Najaf for many years, longer than mujtahids gener-

---

51 Chibli Mallat, "Iraq," in Hunter, *Politics*, p. 78.

ally teach. Al-Khu'i reputedly enjoyed teaching. Unlike al-Hakim, who devoted himself to "running his marja'iya," particularly in terms of addressing political issues, al-Khu'i surrounded himself with students when he was well into his eighties. Because of his long tenure as a teacher, al-Khu'i had more students than any other mujtahid in modern times, and in the hawza students are loyal to their teacher. These students spread al-Khu'i's marja'iya far and wide. And where al-Khu'i's marja'iya spread, Khomeini's was stopped. There was another reason for al-Khu'i being more popular than Khomeini. While both men were Iranian by nationality, al-Khu'i became identified with Iraq. As one person put it, he became "symbolically Arab," while Khomeini's nationalistic feelings about Iran were too evident to gloss over.

It might have been expected that Khomeini would have formed an alliance with the political activitst Muhammad Baqir al-Sadr, yet a number of informants who were in Najaf while Khomeini lived there insist that he had no contact with Baqir al-Sadr. Other sources say that al-Sadr paid Khomeini a visit in Najaf.

Visits between maraji' are extremely uncommon and require considerable attention to protocol. A mujtahid claiming to be a marja' would be placing himself in an inferior position by visiting the home or office of another person claiming the title. If the maraji' have to meet, they select a neutral place for such a meeting. For example, when Ayatollahs Khomeini, Mar'ashi-Najafi, Shari'atmadari, and Gulpaygani met in Iran, it is reported that they met in the home of Muntaziri, who had recognized Khomeini as Iran's spiritual leader and as such was not placing himself on a level with the other grand ayatollahs. Another acceptable meeting site would be the home of the late Ayatollah Ha'iri-Yazdi, the founder of the hawza at Qom. While the home passed to his son, a prominent 'alim in his own right, it also was considered something of an institution, thereby making it an ideal meeting place.

The fact that there was little or no interaction between Baqir al-Sadr and Khomeini, therefore, should not be a surprise in view of the fact that the maraji' do not generally even visit one another, let alone engage in cooperative efforts. However, it might have been expected that, since both al-Sadr and Khomeini devoted themselves to the establishment of an Islamic government, the usual restraints of custom might have been put aside, but my informants state emphatically that Khomeini did not involve himself in the Iraqi Islamist movements. So long as he was free to attack the Iranian government from Iraqi soil, he did not, at least publicly, denounce Iraq. This is not to imply that he supported Iraq at the time. The Iran-Iraq War revealed the antipathy he held for the Ba'thists. However, this hatred was fostered by Saddam's agreement with Iran to force Khomeini's exile from Iraq and Saddam's harsh persecution of the Iraqi Shi'a and the expulsion of Iranians from Iraq after Khomeini was evicted from that country.

Indicative of the lack of close relations between Khomeini and the leading light of Islamic revivalism in Iraq, Imam Baqir al-Sadr, is the correspondence between al-Sadr and Khomeini after the Islamic Revolution. Chibli Mallat has published letters that Khomeini wrote to al-Sadr in which the former addresses the latter as "Hujjat al-Islam," not as "Ayatollah" al-Sadr.[52] The letters certainly do not suggest that the two were working in any kind of collaboration. Mallat also alludes to the fact that Khomeini did not offer hospitality to al-Sadr when trouble broke out in Iraq and when al-Sadr should have been able to expect his protection. However, with Khomeini's success in Iran, he saw an opportunity to export his revolution to Iraq through Baqir al-Sadr. In chapter four I discuss the role of Tehran and the Iranian Arabic newscast in influencing events in Iraq. It will suffice at this point to say that that important factions of the Iraqi Shi'a population hold Khomeini and others close to him at least partially responsible for the death of al-Sadr. The accusers actually include Iraqis who were not active supporters of al-Sadr.

Tehran radio, controlled by Muhammad Shirazi, founder of the Iraqi Islamic 'Amal Movement, and his followers, called upon al-Sadr to rise up against Saddam. Followers of Baqir al-Sadr blame Shirazi, who, it should be recalled, had an adversarial relationship with al-Sadr, for having precipitated as al-Sadr's execution by the Iraqi government. And, since Khomeini ruled Iran, he also is considered culpable. They believe that Radio Tehran's call to arms in Iraq "forced" Saddam to preempt a Shi'i revolution against his own government. How much this played into the execution of Baqir al-Sadr is not clear. Baqir al-Sadr did not attempt to hide his revolutionary zeal and his desire to overthrow the Ba'thists in order to build an Islamic state.

Resentment towards Khomeini by activist Iraqis is often a bit muted. This reflects some of the ambivalence experienced by a people who admire the fact that Khomeini overthrew the Western secular-oriented Shah and established a Shi'i government but who resent what could be seen as his disregard for the Iraqi Shi'a and the disrespect that Khomeini as head of the Iranian government showed towards al-Khu'i. At one point he even froze al-Khu'i's assets in Iran, though the money was released when another ayatollah intervened. Typically, there is a thread

---

52 Chibli Mallat, The Renewal of Islamic Law: Muhammad Baqer As-Sadr, Najaf, and the Shi'i International (Cambridge: Cambridge University Press, 1993), p. 52.

that remains unbroken among the maraji' and their close group. Relations are rarely totally broken.

In his *Will and Testament* Khomeini ignored the existence of the Iraqi Shi'a, while mentioning Shi'a of other nationalities. The sentiment is expressed by at least some Iraqis who say that he never forgave the Iraqi Shi'a for not rising up to fight for Iran against Saddam and thereby allowing Iran's bitter defeat. When Khomeini died in 1989, an Iraqi who is involved in one of the major opposition groups shrugged his shoulders and commented, "we all have to die sometime," thus expressing, at best, rather tepid feelings towards one who might have been considered a fellow Shi'i activist.

Khomeini's Contribution to the Development of Religious Leadership

While he failed to defeat Saddam either through warfare or the revolt of the Shi'i Iraqi population, Khomeini was definitely successful in his attempt to transform Iran into a Shi'i republic. He led Iran on the basis of religious authority, as the representative of the Twelfth Imam. In Iran he was recognized as the marja' taqlid, in spite of al-Khu'i's prominence in the rest of the Shi'i world. Of course, he is renownd for having done something that no other Shi'i leader had ever done: he linked the traditional role of the marja' to temporal political power through his interpretation of the theory of the wilayat al-faqih. However, in Khomeini's case, it was neither office nor theory that truly mattered. What was crucial to his success was his *personal* charisma and his ability to manipulate religious symbols. He became a larger than life figure, even to Shi'a who were not muqallid to him. Both ulama and other Shi'a living outside of Iran often refer to him as Shi'ism's "banner carrier."

Yet, there were other important ulama in Iran, some of whom were recognized as being more knowledgeable than Khomeini, people such as Mar'ashi-Najafi, Shari'atmadari, and Gulpaygani. Sayyid Mahmud Taleghani, while a leader in Tehran, and not in the hawza of Qom, was an important revolutionary clerical figure. However, Khomeini came to surpass them all in power and prestige. Those who challenged Khomeini were removed from the scene in one way or another: either discredited, or placed under house arrest, or killed. While perhaps in the short run Khomeini's actions to silence his high-ranking critics led to his consolidation of leadership, in the long run they are responsible for irreperable damage to the very institution he wished to strengthen.

It will be enlightening to look briefly at Khomeini's treatment of his adversaries and competitors and the effects of these actions.

Khomeini and the Iranian Ayatollahs

Hamid Dabashi gives a brief historical account of the life of Taleghani and his contributions to the revolution.[53] A man who had been at odds with the Pahlavis virtually all of his life, he is referred to as "the Father of the Revolution." Scorning the quietist ulama who dominated Qom at the time, he spent years in exile and in prison. Dabashi recounts the outpouring of emotion at the funeral of Taleghani, referring to him as the "revolutionary father of a whole generation."[54] He threw his prestige behind Khomeini, calling upon the huge crowds that he drew to follow Khomeini as their leader. In an interview with a man who had participated actively in the overthrow of the Shah's regime, this great affection and admiration is again reflected. "He was a very mature, humane person, a very sincere person. After he died, the revolution became very shallow." In spite of Taleghani's enormous popularity—or possibly because of it—his sons were arrested, one of whom was involved with the Mojahedin-e Khalq. According to this same Iranian informant, after these arrests, Taleghani went into the mountains to protest, but was then given an ultimatum by Khomeini. He had to go on television and state that he accepted Khomeini and the welayat al-faqih. Otherwise, he would be declaring jihad on Khomeini. According to the words of this informan, "Taleghani came to TV, and everyone could see he was heavy hearted. He said he believed that Khomeini was the wali faqih and that Khomeini was his Imam." He suffered a fatal heart attack soon after that.

Unlike Taleghani, Shari'atmadari was not a revolutionary, but a reformer. Not a leader among those eager to depose the Shah, he was nevertheless a revered figure in the traditional role of ayatollah and as a marja' taqlid for many Iranians, particularly those in Tabriz and its vicinity. Aside from Ayatollah al-Khu'i, Shari'atmadari was the most revered grand ayatollah in the Shi'i world. Shari'atmadari's moderate views clashed with Khomeini's, something that the latter could not accept. Probably more important was the fact that Shari'atmadari had a following independent of Khomeini, as indeed had Taleghani. It has been said that, if Shari'atmadari had wished to do so, he could have signaled an all-out rebellion against Khomeini in Tabriz. The Tabrizis, in fact, were reportedly awaiting word from him to fight. But he never sent word. This octogenarian, a marja' taqlid to millions of people, appeared on television, a broken man weeping and apologetic. His death, which followed soon after the televised apology, was largely ignored. He was buried

[53] Dabashi, *Theology*, pp. 271–72.

[54] Dabashi, *Theology*, p. 271.

without a proper funeral, a fact that makes thoughtful Shi'a today express great shame.

The links between Ayatollah Khomeini and Ayatollah Muntaziri were far stronger than those between Khomeini and the other ayatollahs. Khomeini and Muntaziri had both been engaged in the struggle against the Shah's White Revolution, and so from the beginning of the revolution Muntaziri's position had been established. Very loyal to Khomeini, he was the leader's heir apparent. Akhavi states that the Council of Experts, elected in 1982 specifically to select Khomeini's successor, had chosen Ayatollah Muntaziri.[55] Yet he too had his own arena separate from Khomeini. He was considered as the marja' for the Isfahan region. From a revolutionary standpoint, his credentials were impeccable. "True radicals," such as the students who occupied the American Embassy in 1979, followed Muntaziri. In spite of these credentials of Muntaziri, Khomeini rescinded this decision shortly before his death in 1989. It is usually stated that Muntaziri was in dispute with Khomeini about human rights, portraying him as a modern reformer. Other informants have pointed out, though, that Muntaziri was the leading figure in Qom when Shari'atmadari died, suggesting that he was implicated in the Ayatollah's death. How concerned he was with the rights of people is in question. However, we do know that he came to the defense of Mahdi Hashimi. Depending on one's viewpoint, he is either the "most sincere element left from among the revolutionaries" or he is "a real murderer." While Muntaziri was in favor with Khomeini, many clerics who opposed their tactics and ideology were under house arrest, casting doubts on his reputation as an ardent supporter of human rights. Muntaziri lived under virtual house arrest for years. Despite what one might feel about Muntaziri, the fact remains that he was the marja' for many people in Isfahan who were no longer legally permitted to make taqlid to him.

After falling out with Muntaziri, Khomeini seems to have recognized that succession would be a problem, so as Abrahamian[56] points out, he modified his theory of wilayat al-faqih shortly before he died. Khomeini divided the clergy into religious specialists and "political" specialists, thereby acknowledging that running a state was not the same as being a religious guide. Still, the head of state was supposed to be a cleric, so he had not not abandoned the idea of a clerically-run government. He did

[55] Akhavi, Shahrough. "State Formation and Consolidating in Twentieth-Century Iran: The Reza Shah Period and the Islamic Republic," in Ali Banuazizi and Myron Weiner, *The State, Religion, and Ethnic Politics: Afghanistan, Iran, and Pakistan* (Syracuse, N.Y.: Syracuse University Press, 1986), p. 213.

[56] Abrahamian, *Khomeinism*, pp. 34–35.

not divide the role of marja' and wali faqih at the end of his life; rather, he redefined the type of person who should serve in this dual capacity.

His modifications were not enough to rid the Iranian regime of succession problems, especially when considering the worldwide Shi'i community. First, the marja' would have to reside in Iran. While there is a tendency for Iranians to prefer to emulate a marja' in Iran, the new circumstances of the Islamic Republic would seemingly make this a necessity. As head of state the marja'/wali faqih could not live in Najaf. Second, the institution of the marja'iya, while ever-evolving, had become a strongly entrenched institution that served the spiritual and practical needs of many Shi'a, including ulama supported by the maraji'. Finally, as a powerful personal figure, Khomeini actually weakened the institution. He taught that it was the office that was important, yet his life and the events following his death belied this notion. The institution that he envisioned has proven to be insufficient to wield power. Only if the marja' who exercises wilayat al-faqih as defined by Khomeini has sufficient charisma and prestige can he fill this dual position of religious and temporal leader. However, the great charismatic religious leaders of Iran were not going to fall into line with Khomeini's thinking.

Because there was no acceptable high-ranking mujtahid to succeed Khomeini, the Council of Experts appointed a lower ranking mujtahid, Hujjat al-Islam Khamane'i, as president of the Islamic Republic of Iran. His nomination was promoted by Rafsanjani and Ahmad Khomeini. Khomeini's son Ahmad said that he heard his father refer to Khamene'i as wali faqih, but there seems to have been no widespread use of the term when referring to him, nor was he referred to as a marja' after Khomeini's death. The government—or factions thereof—saw that they would need time to establish the marja'iya of Khamene'i and needed someone to fill the role in the interim. The Islamic Republic faced the dilemma of putting a cleric lacking in traditional credentials for the institution of the marja' into this office or allowing someone outside the government to hold this it. The latter solution posed a danger because a person recognized as a marja' could be anti-government and incite people to speak out against governmental policies. It attempted to solve its problem by putting forward a very old mujtahid, Ayatollah Araki. Araki was an ideal choice for the Islamic Republic—offering them a blank check, so to speak, as well as the time needed to build the stature of Khamene'i and raise his credibility within the religious establishment and the masses at large. Essentially Araki said that everyone could continue to follow Khomeini's fatwas and that he would disagree with none of them. Most important, he sanctioned the theory of wilayat al-faqih. He also promised not to replace any of the ulama who served as imam jum'a, the Friday prayer leaders, as they had formed an elite group in Iran and were jealous of their positions.

The senior members of the government, in spite of its propoganda to the contrary, did not have as much say over the marja'iya as they would have liked. It is as if they themselves did not understand the basic ideas of the marja'iya. The government, with its large clerical component, should have known that so long as a highly respected and revered mujtahid is still alive, the majority of people feel an obligation to follow him in preference to a less distinguished 'alim. Al-Khu'i outlived Khomeini, so therefore even Khomeini's followers felt obligated to follow him in preference to Khamene'i, adding to his already enormous prestige. When al-Khu'i died in 1992, another prominent Iranian mujtahid still lived, Ayatollah Sabzevari. For many years Sabzevari had had a following among people from his home province of Azerbaijan, even when he was living in the shadow of other more prominent maraji'. The Islamic Republic authorities attempted to ignore al-Khu'i and Sabzevari, both of whom resided in Najaf, and others over whom they would have no control, but the idea of putting forward an 'alim with no reputation worth speaking of as a marja', especially while genuinely qualified people were alive, was unacceptable to most people. Of course, there were some who were willing to follow any candidate the government put forward, such as a group of Iranian students living in the United States were interviewed after Khomeini's death. However, most people, Iranian or not, refused to follow Araki even after the deaths of al-Khu'i and Sabzevari.

There was another strong contender for the role, someone to whom many had been muqallid throughout the years of Khomeini and al-Khu'i. This was Ayatollah Gulpaygani. He it was who had prayed over the body of Khomeini at his funeral, in spite of the fact that he had not accepted Khomeini's theory of wilayat al-faqih.[57] As mentioned above, praying at the funeral of the deceased marja' is an indication that one has been recognized as the marja''s successor by other high-ranking ulama and that he has accepted that recognition. Gulpaygani also reportedly had even more students than al-Khu'i. His one disadvantage had been living at the time of the revolution, which Khomeini had led, but apparently there came a time when even the Iranian government could not prevent him from becoming the grand marja' for most of the Shi'a world. The government simply could not override public sentiment. They did not interfere with his marja'iya—but nor did they allow him to have any direct impact on the state.

How Gulpaygani's rose to the position is interesting and shows the

[57] Akhavi, "State Formation," p. 218.

complications of becoming a grand marja'. In a newsletter published by the International Islamic Society of Virginia, an article about Ayatullah Gulpaygani begins with the announcement of the Ayatollah's death at the age of ninety-six: "His demise, which took place a short period after his elevation to the highest religious rank in Shi'a Islam, namely that of Marja' Taqlid A'la, sent shock waves throughout the Muslim world in general and the Shi'a world in particular." The writer states that Gulpaygani was "Marja' Taqlid for 32 years, spending 70 years of his life at Qum teaching Islamics." Further on, the article relates that on July 16, 1993,

> the Central Committee of the Imam Al-Khoei Islamic Foundation met in London to decide what to do, in as far as the management of the Foundation is concerned, in the wake of the demise of the Foundations's founder and patron. It was decided that the said Committee should act upon Article 5 of the Foundation's Bylaws. The said article indicates that in the event of the death of Imam Al-Khoei, the Board of Directors of the Foundation will have to be entrusted to the capable hands of the marja' who is widely believed to have the most following. The said Committee, therefore, submitted a written request signed by all its board members requesting His Late holiness Ayatullah al-Uzma Gulpaygani to graciously accept the responsibility of supervizing the world-wide Islamic activities of the said Foundation, a request to which he, may Allah rest his soul in peace, responded favorably.

This suggests the ambiguity of the position of marja' taqlid. While Gulpaygani was referred to as a marja' for many years, according to the official announcement of his death, he had been elevated to that position only shortly before he died. No exact date of elevation could be given, but it is obvious that it refers to anytime between a few months and a few years and not the thirty-two years referred to in the article. The other interesting point revealed here is how the Al-Khoei Foundation selected their marja'. Essentially, the marja' was chosen by a committee and, while some of its members are ulama, they are not the world's leading ulama. Their role as ulama is really secondary to their role as officers of the Foundation. The article indicates that they met in July of 1993, only five months before the death of Gulpaygani. By then, Gulpaygani had been accepted very widely as a supreme marja', though his fame as a marja' was certainly nothing like that of al-Khu'i or Khomeini. Why they might have waited so long before endorsing Gulpaygani will be discussed later. For now, it will suffice to say that they did not rush to proclaim Gulpaygani's marja'iya, but rubber-stamped a decision others had made. These others would not have been the members of the government of the Islamic Repubic, for there never had been close relations between those affiliated with al-Khu'i and those who had backed Khomeini. Obviously, the process of agreeing on Gulpaygani was a complicated and tortuous trek.

Let us return to the succession of religious leadership in Iran. After Gulpaygani's death, the government once again promoted Araki as the supreme marja'. With the death of Gulpaygani, the hawza in Qom had lost its greatest mujtahid, and there was no one left in Iran with his stature. Therefore, the resistence to Araki this time would not be so strong. Since he was well into his nineties at this point, Araki was was so ineffectual that calling him the marja' could have little consequence for anyone. Araki died about a year after Gulpaygani, so there was no time to test whether his marja'iya would spread or not. It is unlikely that it would have. There is no indication that he had been working to establish his reputation as a jurist. It seems that Araki will be remembered only for his banning of satellite dishes.

As long as Gulpaygani and Araki were alive, the government could postpone a real crisis. At the time of Araki's death, there was a new generation of mujtahids who, while lacking the status of a Khu'i or Gulpaygani, were far enough advanced in rank and age to be considered contenders for the office. There was something of a generation gap in the process of developing new leadership. This was due to the policies of Reza Shah's twenty-year reign during which he prevented people from rising through the madrasa system to the rank of marja'. When Khomeini and Gulpaygani, who were peers, died, there were no obvious candidates waiting in the wings to fill their role from the next generation. However, by the mid-1990s there were several men who were all in the same age range—in their sixties and seventies—who had risen through the system at approximately the same time. Some of these men were traditional religious scholars; others were activists. The most outstanding of the latter group were at odds with the Iranian government, namely Muntaziri, Muhammad Shirazi, and Muhammad Ruhani.

There were others as well, who, while not part of the open opposition, did not openly support the government either. While the government has not actively suppressed this latter group, they also did not want to encourage them. What the government wanted was a strong candidate of their own who could overshadow any of these other mujtahids. Therefore, they put forward President 'Ali Khamene'i as the senior religious leader. The government was not just proposing that Khamene'i should be the grand marja'; it was also nominating him as the person who would merge the marja'iya with political leadership. He was nowto be the wali faqih.

It is interesting to see how the government, or rather some factions of it, went about pushing Khamene'i's temporal/religious leadership. First,

Khamene'i is generally considered to be a hujjat al-Islam—i.e., an aspiring mujtahid, and, consequently, not high ranking enough to be considered a marja'.[58] Khamene'i has never produced a risala, though he has written a book referred to as *Questions and Answers*. One 'alim explained that Khamene'i had decided to write in this form rather than produce a risala because writing "a real risalah" would have shown the senior ulama quite plainly the inferior quality of his learning.

The factions of the government supporting Khamene'i reflect Khomeini's view that, in these days, the greatest necessity for the role is knowledge of world affairs, something that they protested Khamene'i had in abundance. This did not quell public dissent, so the government instructed the Association of Teachers at the Qom theological seminary to select seven men who were eligible candidates for the role of marja'.[59] The list I was shown is as follows: Nasir Makra Shirazi, 'Ali Khamene'i, Wahid Khorasani, Fadl Lankarani, Mirza Taqi Baghdadi, Jawad Tabrizi, and Musawi Zanjani. Each of these individuals had to receive at least seven votes to be on the list. With Khamene'i's name on the list, the government could go ahead and continue to promote his marja'iya, using a variety of tactics. For example, at the funeral of Ayatollah Khomeini a first-hand witness says that Khamene'i prayed behind Gulpaygani. This witness, a madrasa-educated Iranian who also has an ijaza from Fadlallah and an avowed supporter of Khamene'i's marja'iya says, "This is something that will never happen again." Of course, everyone present would know that Gulpaygani was "superior" in rank to Khamene'i . He was recognized as the grand marja' in Iran and elsewhere. However, this mulla's statement was meant to suggest that, even as early as 1989, Khamene'i was of a higher rank than Gulpaygani. His words imply that Khamene'i was graciously allowing Gulpaygani to have the privilege of presiding at the funeral.

Indeed, this mulla's comment is consistent with the spin that Khamene'i's supporters within Iran have put on his ascendance to the marja' /wali faqih position. In a June 1995 news article entitled "A Brief Biography of Ayatollah Seyyed 'Ali Hussaini Khamene'i, the anonymous writer quotes Khomeini as speaking of Khamene'i as his heir apparent:

> On June 8th, 1989, the first Friday after the demise of Imam Khomeini (RA), Hojatolislam wal Muslimin Hashemi Rafsanjani shared with

58 However, I should note that I have spoken to Khamene'i supporters who do view him as a mujtahid, using the title "ayatollah."

59 For a discussion of the elections and their implications, see Roy, Mottahedeh, "The Islamic Movement: The Case for Democratic Inclusion," *Contention* 4/3 (1995), pp. 107-27.

> the public the discussions which took place in the presence of Imam Khomeini (RA) and Imam's opinion with regard to the best person suited for assuming the position of Wilayat-e Faqih. He said: 'Concerning our dear brother, our new eminent Leader, we repeatedly debated with the Imam over the issue of the deputy leadership (the person who would assume the position of Leadership after the Leader). In one session, the heads of three branches, Ayatollah Ardabili (the head of Judiciary), myself [then speaker of the parliament], the prime minister, and Hajj Ahmad Agha (Imam Khomeini's son) and our present leader the five of us were present. A discussion ensued and we said to the Imam that if this happens we will have difficulties because with the present constitution we could have a leadership vacuum. He said that this would not be the case since we have the right people. When we said who, he pointed to Ayatollah Khamene'i. Following that session, Ayatollah Khamene'i asked us, insisted, that we did not talk about this issue outside. We did not repeat it anywhere. Recenlty, more debate started. I went to his eminience the Imam (RA) privately, because I could speak more openly over the issue of the deputy Leadership and its problems. This time, he told clearly that we would not have any problem because we had such an individual amongst us and we should realize it. This is what happened then. Hajj Hamed Agha also said that while he (Ayatollah Khamene'i) was in North Korea and the Imam (RA) saw him on TV, his meetings, speeches, and discussions, it was very interesting for Imam (RA) who said that 'he is truly worthy of the Leadership.'''

Parallels between this portrayal of Khomeini's appointment of Khamene'i and Shi'i accounts of the Prophet Muhammad's appointment of Imam 'Ali ibn Abi Talib are striking, giving the process of Khamene'i's rise a sense of sacred legitimation. Nonetheless, the elections and the rhetoric have not seemed to be very persuasive. While informants have told me that bazaris have found it advantageous to follow Khamene'i because paying khums to him guarantees his support for their interests, the vast majority of people have opted to be muqallid to local mujtahids, so that, if a person lives in Khurasan, he might follow Ayatollah Qomi, or if in Azerbaijan, Ayatollah Lankarani. People often, though certainly not always, ignore the decisions in Qom.

However, the government has ways to punish those who insist on following a marja' of whom they disapprove, especially one who openly disagrees with the Iranian government. The most prominent of these dissident mujtahids are Ruhani, Muhammad Shirazi, and Muntaziri, all of whom are forces to be reckoned with. Ruhani was conisdered by many to have been al-Khu'i's protégé, but his confinement in Iran has hindered his quest to be recognized as the marja', though he does have followers in Kuwait and the Gulf. Muntaziri, in spite of being at odds with the government, or perhaps because of it, still has a large following in

Iran, including in parliament. A knowledgeable source said that "Muntaziri would certainly be the majra' taqlid in Iran were it not for his poor relationship to the government." The same person commented that Shirazi, because of his "boldness, lack of fear of the government, and knowledge have made him recognized even by deputies in the majlis." In Iran today, a person who is caught being muqallid to any of these men is approached by the Iranian tax authorities and faces fines. Several of Shirazi's followers are in prison, and one was killed in prison in February 1996. Pressure is being applied to Shirazi to make a statement backing the government in its attempt to annoint Khamene'i as the religious/political leader of Iran.

The announcement by the Iranian government that Khamene'i was the next marja' caused considerable dissent both inside and outside of Iran. His lack of credentials was glaring. The hawza could not support him as the greatest faqih of the day, nor could the vast majority of Shi'a. Because of the large-scale rejection of Khamene'i as a marja', the Iranian government changed the law that the wali faqih had to be a marja', clearing the way for Khamene'i to legitimately hold wali faqih position. After hearing the criticism of his candidacy to the marja'iya, Khamene'i himself said that he was not putting himself forward as a marja' inside Iran. However, he declared himself the marja' for the rest of the Shi'i world, based on the fact that he had knowledge of the world that other mujtahids lacked. This seems to have been a major diplomatic mistake. Complaints were heard among Shi'a living in the United States that the Iranians got to choose their own marja', but the rest of the Shi'a could not! Because the Iranian people at large did not fall in line behind Khamene'i, the Iranian government began saying that it is perfectly all right to have many maraji', stating that it is a point of pride to have so many high-ranking, knowledgeable ulama, although they certainly have not given up on promoting their candidate. They have not given up on their quest to see Khamene'i as the world-recognized marja' taqlid and are actively pursuing their goal of establishing his reputation.

One Iranian cleric living abroad speculated that in five years or so the situation will be different. In that time, the people will come to know more about the mujtahids who are eligible to be considered as maraji'. He did not see this as an unhealthy situation at all. Khomeini, he said, laid the foundation, and now it is simply a matter of a qualified person taking the helm. That person will, according to this cleric, emerge in the near future. He should perhaps not feel so sanguine. The linking of temporal and spiritual leadership, the direct government involvement in the selection process, the legal measures taken against those who follow the "wrong" marja', and the use of sahm al-Imam as a virtual slush fund all serve to detract from the sacredness of the institution. In a December 13, 1994, article in *The Independent,* the exiled former Iranian president Bani Sadr is quoted as saying, "Reza Shah ended forever the 2,500-year old Iranian monarchy because he destroyed the very foundations and traditions of the monarchy. Now, it is Khamene'i's turn to destroy the post of marja." Any mujtahid who rises to a high position now is suspect because he must be approved by the government in order to be considered a marja'. Thus, he can be associated with all the errors and misdeeds of the regime. It is possible that a marja' in the traditional sense—a person confined to religious scholarship and piety—could arise as the chief clerical figure, but the government has already taken measures to ensure that, so long as the people will not accept "their man," there will be numerous maraji', no one of whom can in any way be a threat to them.

As mentioned above, having a marja' outside of Iran would be highly problematic for the Islamic Republic. As the government actively promotes Khamene'i's marja'iya and tries to consolidate its power, the prospect of Iranian and other Shi'a following a marja' outside of Iran has become a knottier problem than ever. Iran, as the only country in the world with a Shi'i government, could not tolerate having its supreme religious leaders outside Iran and outside its control. A mujtahid in opposition within Iran is a serious enough problem, but at least the government can monitor and control his actions. They cannot exert such direct control over someone outside Iran. That they actively try to dissuade Iranians from looking elsewhere for a marja' is indicated in a report by the Federal News Service on November 30, 1994: "Khamene'i had earlier said the 'enemies of Iran and the Shi'ites' were conspiring to bring in a non-Iranian to the post [marja' taqlid] and vowed that Tehran would not stand for that."

Refusing the Role of Marja'

While the marja' is supposed to be the most learned and most just mujtahid of the age, it does not necessarily follow that the person who truly is the most learned and just will wish to be the marja'. Just as there are qualified individuals who might win the presidency in the United States but choose not to run, so too there are mujtahids who decline to be considered for the marja'iya. One elderly, prominent 'alim spoke about Wahid Khurasani as probably being the most highly qualified mujtahid to be a marja' but refused to "declare himself" as such. Speaking about Khurasani, this 'alim said, "Because of the sensitivity of the issue of the marja'iya in Iran with Khamene'i, etc., he backed down from claiming to be a marja'. He is renowned for usul al-fiqh and 'irfan. There are people who follow him but are quiet about it. He wrote a fatwa that khums is not wajib (mandatory) to pay. Even if he had declared himself a marja', he would not collect khums."

Even in the best of times, the marja'iya carries responsibilities that not everyone might want. A person who has pursued theological and legal studies in the Shi'i madrasas, a process that involves knowing a great many pedantic details, might understandably be reclusive in temperament. Yet, as we have seen with al-Khu'i, a constant procession of people wishing to visit and question is part and parcel of the life of a marja'. The marja', even with a great deal of assistance from sons and sons-in-law, has to forfeit a life of seclusion and reflection as he spends his days answering queries and meeting with guests and officials. The political situation in the Middle East has added tremendously to the burdens of the marja'. Governmental interference in the institution has intensified, so that danger for one's life can be included in the list of disadvantages of being a marja' taqlid

In the following chapters we will see how governmental actions have affected the institution of the marja'iya. Aside from sharpening the divide between the "political" and "apolitical" ulama, the actions of the Iranian government have generated renewed debates among various strata of Shi'i society on the role of the marja' and how it should be structured. Current conditions have also intensified a sense of Iranian vs. non-Iranian Shi'ism in the world. All of these issues are magnified by the fact that so many Shi'a have left the Middle East to live in the West, so that, in addition to redefining the marja'iya, they are also redefining themselves in relation to the rest of the world. We will see how these processes intertwine.

Chapter Five

The Martyred Marja'

I FIRST NOTICED THE NAME of Ayatollah Muhammad-Baqir al-Sadr when I moved to a Shi'ite Lebanese neighborhood in Dearborn, Michigan. As I bought boooks from the excellent Arabic bookstore there, I noticed that his books were almost all in stock: highly respected treatments of both traditional and modern religious topics. The msoques sold them, as well. Two works especially were vernated by my educated Shi'ite friends: *Our Philosophy* and *Our Economics.* The reason for this was obvious. They were erudite attempts to justify conservative Islam as a serious idological alternative to Marxism and democratic capitalism. Some months later I attended a memorial meeting at one of the local mosques commemorating the ninth anniversary of his death. The speakers were a panel of Shi'ite clerics ranging from the mosque imam and a reciter of the sufferings of Husayn to erudite scholars from Najaf. Each spoke at length of 'this great clergyman.' Each portrayed him as a giant of Islam, whether the Islam of piety or of scholarship or of revolution. Here, I thought, was an intellectual figure worthy of notice.[60]

WITH THESE WORDS, John Walbridge, a scholar of Islamic philosophy, began a paper that he presented at a Middle East Studies conference in 1991. Baqir al-Sadr's appeal to Western scholars is not difficult to

[60] "Muhammad-Baqir al-Sadr on Induction: The Critique of Rationalism and Empiricism and the New Theory of Probability," presented at the 1990 annual meeting of the Middle East Studies Association.

understand. First, he had a deep interest in Western thought and addressed the practical needs of the modern world while attempting to remain true to his religious principles. Second, his sister, Bint al-Huda, who was obviously loved and admired by al-Sadr, advocated for women to be educated and actively involved in the world. She was the archetypal Islamic feminist. Finally, Baqir al-Sadr and his sister were brutally executed by Saddam Hussein's regime the year following Khomeini's rise to power. Eventually, Saddam Hussein's name would become synonomous with brutality and the inhumane treatment of Kurds and Shi'ites alike. Perhaps equally important, though, Baqir al-Sadr never had a chance to tarnish his image, at least in the eyes of the West. He could remain the erudite reformer, the seeker of common ground between East and West. One could label him "the Khomeini of Iraq," yet there are no images of him lambasting America, no televised tirades against "the Great Satan." Saddam had him killed before any negative associations could be attached to his name. The West—or at least those in the West who have heard of Baqir al-Sadr—can accept him as a martyr.

Next to Khomeini, Baqir al-Sadr is probably the most widely known Shi'i cleric in modern history. In fact, he is commonly referred to as Iraq's Khomeini. His reputation has spread in the West through his early book, *Our Philosophy,* which was translated into English.[61] Because he addresses contemporary issues and directly engages ideologies that sprang from the West, his writings have been used as a way to counter criticisms of Islam. Baqir al-Sadr's popularity has spread to young Sunni activists as his most widely read works do not emphasize Shi'ism and thus have wider appeal than Shi'i works usually have. Baqir al-Sadr's martyrdom, his notoriety among American scholars, commemorative services such as the one described above, and the use of his writings among non-Shi'i Muslims might lead one to believe that he would be universally revered among the Shi'a.

However, the dynamics of clerical politics seem to preclude the possibility that such a person as Baqir al-Sadr would enjoy universal adulation in Najaf and the other holy cities. Chibli Mallat hints that all was not well between Khomeini and Baqir al-Sadr by quoting letters in which Khomeini diminished Baqir al-Sadr's station, addressing him as "hojjat al-Islam" rather than as "ayatollah." One might dismiss Khomeini's behavior as simply Iranian/Iraqi rivalry. However, upon further inspection, it seems that Baqir al-Sadr was and is as controversial a figure as one could hope to find. Baqir al-Sadr, in fact, seems to be the focal point for much

---

61 *Falsafatunā,* many editions; *Our Philosophy,* trans. Shams C. Inati (London: Muhammadi Trust and KPI, 1987).

of the ambivalence, doubt, and guilt that permeates the clerical class of Iraq.

In this chapter we will explore the career of Baqir al-Sadr, his life, his ideas, and his times, all of which help to elucidate the process by which a junior mujtahid rises to prominence in religous circles. We also get a glimpse of the competition in the hawza for the marja'iya. Ultimately, though, as we will see, many questions remain unanswered. Baqir al-Sadr's life and his death are shrouded in mystery. In a sense, the mystery is inevitable and reflects the nature of the marja'iya. It underscores the ephemeral quality of the institution—a quality that Baqir al-Sadr himself wished to obliterate. Every interview conducted about Baqir al-Sadr produces a different picture—either about the man himself or about the circumstances that led to his death.

Baqir al-Sadr's Life and Career

Muhammad Baqir al-Sadr was born in 1936 in the Shi'ite shrine neighborhood of Kazimayn in northern Baghdad. He came from an illustrious clerical family, his father being himself an ayatollah and his cousin the famous Imam Musa al-Sadr, the founder of Harakat Amal in Lebanon. By the 1960s Muhammad Baqir al-Sadr was well recognized as an intellectual force in the hawza of Najaf. While our sources leave no doubt whatsoever that he participated in the establishment of al-Da'wa al-Islamiya (the Islamic Preaching), there are those who have questioned it. The fact that there is this discrepancy is in and of itself interesting. There is good reason to believe that those who deny al-Sadr's activities in al-Da'wa were linked to al-Majlis al-A'la (SCIRI, the Supreme Council of the Islamic Revolution in Iraq), which is Iranian-based and at odds with al-Da'wa. In the 1980s when there was much animosity between Al-Da'wa and SCIRI, SCIRI members who wished to discredit al-Da'wa might not want to besmirch Baqir al-Sadr's name in the process as he was the most visible symbol of Iraqi religious resistance to the Iraqi regime. For anyone actively fighting the Iraqi regime, the martyred mujtahid could be called forth as a hero to emulate, whether or not one was directly linked to him.

Be that as it may, Mahdi al-Hakim, the son of the late Ayatollah Muhsin al-Hakim, stated in an interview in *Shahada,* the official paper of SCIRI, that Talib al-Rifa'i, a close friend of al-Sadr's who had long been politically active and associated with the Tahrir party, asked al-Sadr to head al-Da'wa. By this time, al-Rifai, Mahdi al-Hakim, and Sahib Dakhil, the head figure of al-Da'wa known also as Abu 'Isam, had formed the first cell and were looking for a major clerical figure to give them religious legitimacy. Al-Sadr was chosen by this group to be the

Faqih al-Hizb, the jurist of the party, in 1958, indicating that even this early he had gained a reputation in the hawza (though as we will see below, not a high rank) in spite of his youth. According to Talib al-Rifa'i, Mahdi al-Hakim and A. Hadi al-Fadhli, all top leaders in al-Da'wa, al-Sadr was the one who actually chose the name of the party, al-Da'wa al-Islamiya. He was also credited as being the sole author of the Usus, the party's main political doctrine. According to M. Baqir al-Nasiri, a well-known Iraqi religious figure, al-Sadr once came to him with Mahdi al-Hakim to recruit him to al-Da'wa, again reaffirming his active involvement.

It should be clarified that, in the absence of a Shi'i political organization prior to the formation of al-Da'wa, it was common for the politically motivated jurists or Islamists to join Sunni organizations, such as Tahrir and Ikhwan, despite the theological differences between the two sects. Yet, ultimately, the Shi'i ulama and Islamists left the Sunni organizations due to theological disputes. For example, the publication of the pamphlet, *al-Khalifa*, by the Tahrir party advocating the Sunni view of the succession to leadership after the death of the Prophet made many Shi'i Islamists desert the party and begin one of their own. The need for such a party was underscored by the rapid spread of communism among the Iraqi Shi'a after the 1958 Revolution. The formation of al-Da'wa was initially simply a response to the threat that communism posed to religion in Iraq. It was not part of a strategic plan to achieve longterm political goals. Al-Da'wa was not the only attempt to offset the communist threat. Prior to al-Da'wa's inception, a group of high-ranking mujtahids formed the Jama'at al-'Ulama for this purpose. Although it was short lived, al-Sadr had probably gained credentials as an activist through this organization, as he had played a pivotal role by editing its main journal, *al-Adwa'* (The Lights), and drafting its leaflets and political statements. It is indicative of the social structure of the hawza that, in spite of his efforts on behalf of the organization, he was considered too low-ranking at the time to be an official member.

While in the party he was exposed to the political writings of the main leftist and Sunni political parties that had been active in Iraq since the 1950s. The influence from the ideology of these parties is apparent. For example, the al-Da'wa borrowed Tahrir's doctrine of gradual political change in an attempt to establish an Islamic government. From the leftist parties al-Da'wa took the idea of forming clandestine cells to safeguard against political repression. Al-Sadr was largely responsible for drafting the al-Da'wa program, borrowing from ideas of Lenin and even the hated Ba'th party itself.

Sadr gained real fame when he published his books *Falsafatuna* (Our

Philosophy) and *Iqtisaduna* (Our Economics). It is these works that catapulted him into fame among young Muslim activists in Iraq and throughout the Middle East. The acclaim he won for these books surprised al-Sadr himself. Still only in twenties and living in an environment that revered age, he had originally wanted to publish his treatises under the name of Jama'at al-'Ulama, which, as mentioned earlier, was limited to older, well-established mujtahids. According to Kazim al-Ha'iri, he is reported to have commented that "had he thought *Fasafatuna* would earn him such immediate prominence, this might have affected his ego."[62]

Criticism from Within

The acclaim that al-Sadr earned from young intellectuals and activists was offset by the disapproval he received from within the hawza itself. The hawza of Najaf was noted for its apolitical stance, the exception to this rule being the marja'iya of Muhsin al-Hakim. Al-Hakim's marja'iya was considered a breakthrough by those wishing to see the Shi'a addressing political issues. After the failure of the 1920 revolt against the British-backed monarchy, in which the Shi'i mujtahids had played a leading role, the five leading religious leaders in Iraq were expelled from the country to Iran or India. Eventually four of them were allowed to return on the condition that they not interfere in Iraqi internal afffairs. The only one who would not accept these conditions was Shaykh Mahdi al-Khalisi of Kazimayn, who preferred exile in India to a "sellout" of the Iraqi Shi'a. Among the four who did sign were Mirza Na'ini, the a leading figure of the Constititonal movement of Iran.[63] His book, *Tanbih al-Umma wa Tanzih al-Milla* (Warning to the Islamic community and purification of the nation), a tract supporting the Iranian Constitutional Revolution, was first Shi'ite work to introduce the concept of popular sovereignty, i.e., the rights of people to elect their government. Also returning to Najaf was Abu'l-Hasan al-Isfahani, widely recognized in Iraq and among many outside of Iraq as the grand marja' who preceded al-Hakim . These men quietly settled down to teaching jurisprudence rather than politics, producing the likes of Ayatollah al-Khu'i as a result. Thus, al-Hakim's activities seemed quite extraordinary at the time. He began building public libaries, sending representatives to different Iraqi cities, sanctioning religious ceremonies, and, perhaps most remarkable of all, sanctioning political activites, including al-Da'wa and Jama'at al-'Ulama.

Yet al-Da'wa seems to have been seen as too much of a threat by the

---

62 Kāẓim al-Ḥā'irī, *Tarjumat Ḥayāt al-Marja' al-Ṣadr* (Qum, Iran: 1988), p. 159.

63 Nakhash, *Shi'is,* 75–85.

majority of people in the hawza at that time. They could not tolerate a member of their ranks leading a political party whose goal was to lead a revolutionary struggle, even if its goal was to establish an Islamic government. This, they believed, was the role of the Imam Mahdi, not of a jurist in the hawza. The anti-al-Da'wa feelings finally drove some of leading members out of the party. These included Muhsin al-Hakim's sons, Mahdi and Muhammad Baqir. Through his sons, Muhsin al-Hakim pressured al-Sadr to give up his post as faqih of al-Da'wa and editor of *al-Adwa'*, the Jama'at al-'Ulama's main journal, in 1961.[64] Al-Khu'i also pressured al-Sadr to resign and, since he was al-Khu'i's student, al-Sadr couldn't refuse.

Thus, Baqir al-Sadr left al-Da'wa and began his own quest for the marja'iya.

Different Versions of the Story

Not everyone who knew Baqir al-Sadr will agree with this account of his story. Some clerics associated with Muhammad Shirazi question whether or not Baqir al-Sadr was truly a student of al-Khu'i. He was a generation too young, they said, and was actually the student of a student of al-Khu'i, Ayatollah Ruhani in Qom, a marja' taqlid with a growing reputation outside of Iran. Yet friends of al-Sadr who were interviewed say that al-Sadr had only one mentor in fiqh and usul and that was al-Khu'i. Moreover, al-Sadr himself refers to al-Khu'i as "ustadhi" (my teacher). Generally, a student will make reference to the views of his teacher of bahth al-kharij; in al-Sadr's book on usul, *Durus fi Ilm al-Usul,* he mentions only al-Khu'i. It is quite possible that al-Sadr did take courses with Ayatollah Ruhani, but did not view him as a principal teacher. What is interesting is that there are people who are eager to put forward the view that Ruhani was an important influence in al-Sadr's life. Generally, a student gains charisma from his teacher. In this case, the teacher is apparently gaining charisma from his illustrious, martyred student. Though he is a controversial figure, al-Sadr does, unquestionably, have prestige for many Shi'a.

However, there are those who did not admire his work and political activities and actually appear puzzled by his notoriety. As one Iraqi informant with close ties to the hawza in Najaf said,

> In the hawza he was not considered so heroic. There were many like him. He was not exactly average, but the reason that he is famous is because of the translation of his books and the fact that he was involved in

64 Muḥammad-Ḥusayn Faḍlallāh, preface to Muḥammad-Bāqir al-Sadr, *Risālatunā.* Reference not verified.

> politics like Khomeini. Why from all the great mujtahids do people in the West only know Khomeini and Baqir al-Sadr? Baqir al-Sadr established Hizb al-Da'wa. When Khomeini established the Iranian government, Baqir al-Sadr supported him, but before that there was no relationship between the two. He didn't write anything political from 1973 until his death.

There is even the suggestion that when the Ba'thists first came to power in Iraq in 1968, they sought to find a Shi'i leader they could control. Obviously, al-Hakim , who was recognized as the marja' in Iraq at the time, would not be amenable to control. Al-Hakim, by then, had a long history of being at odds with the Iraqi government. According to someone close to the marja'iya, the Iraqi government "looked for a younger man and picked Sayyid Baqir al-Sadr, thinking maybe they could have a good relationship with him. Before that time in Baghdad University the Qur'an was studied through al-Khu'i's book—*al-Bayan*. The government stopped the use of this book and gave them al-Sadr's book instead." Evidently, there were those in the hawza who felt that Baqir al-Sadr had betrayed them, saying that "they had educated Baqir al-Sadr, and he went against us."

A different portrayal of this situation comes from an admirer of Baqir al-Sadr. He states:

> The Ba'thists wanted to rid the education system in Iraq from any religious teaching, emphasizing secular education. I remember when the Ba'thists came to power in 1968, they took religion off the list of required courses needed to pass the high school examination. Religious classes became minor in my high school. Since al-Sadr's books give the best intellectual attack against communism [the enemy of the Ba'thist, Arab nationalist, ideolology] and capitalism, they would have found his books on economics and philosophy more appealing than the traditional religious books. When *Falsafatuna* was first published in Lebanon in 1959, it was the Ba'thist newspaper in Baghdad which did a review of the book and started publishing sections of it that were critical of communist ideology. It was an unholy aliance between the Islamists and the Ba'thists to counter communism which was on the ascendance after the 1958 revolution.

Even Talib al-Rifa'i, a friend of Baqir al-Sadr, said in a personal interview that the Islamists used to participate with members of the Ba'th party in publishing and distributing leaflets that attacked communism. Yet, this early "cooperation" between Baqir al-Sadr's people and the Ba'thists is interpreted by Baqir al-Sadr's supporters as being similar to other struggles in which opposing sides temporarily come together to fight a mutually-hated foe. In neighboring Iran, the goal of overthrowing the Shah brought about temporary alliances among a variety of competing groups who later fought one another.

Yet, it is obvious that some Iraqis—including clerics—prefer the more unflattering portrayal of al-Sadr as a conspirator working with Saddam. Why might this be? A clue might be found in an article by Muhammad al-Husayni, "al-Imam al-Sadr," in which the author cites instances when al-Khu'i's people collaborated with the Ba'th regime. Indeed, informants have directly stated that there was a cooperative relationship between Saddam and al-Khu'i until the end. One person stated that Saddam even visited al-Khu'i in the middle of the night. While such a relationship might have been seen as expedient at the time, at this time, no one wishes to be perceived as having ever worked with Saddam Hussein. The "crime" of cooperation with Saddam might be diminished in the eyes of the people if it is thought that the martyred Baqir al-Sadr had also found occasion when it was beneficial to work with Saddam.

The greatest disagreement concerns the last days of Baqir al-Sadr: whether he had a large following, whether his followers abandoned him or protested his arrests. Baqir al-Sadr was arrested twice. After the first arrest, his sister Bint al-Huda went to the shrine of Imam 'Ali and pleaded with the people to "save your marja'."A demonstration did follow, though what is under dispute is the size and intensity of the protest. The most serious disagreements occur over whether or not an uprising followed al-Sadr's final arrest. One al-Sadr supporter said,

> My brother-in-law was among those who participated in the first demonstration that sparked the uprising. He was tortured for forty days in the Central Security Agency in Baghdad. His life was spared, but fourteen of his schoolmates who participated in the uprising were killed. They took my wife's father to look at them before the execution as a warning to him of the destiny of his son [if he continued in anti-government activities]. My brother-in-law told me how they decided to launch their campaign from al-Khu'is congregational prayer in order to force him to be active against the government. But al-Khu'i issued a fatwa saying that these people were not his *muqallids*. My brother-in-law was al-Khu'is *muqallid*, not al-Sadr's.

This same person said that his father was in Samawa at the time of the uprising and told him that

> students and professionals, government employees, and others held several demonstrations in the central market and went through the major streets in the city. Each time the goverment arrested as many protesters as possible. They started rounding up every young person that prayed in the mosques or had a beard. Samawa lost its only two religious scholars, a representative of al-Sadr and one of al-Khu'i's. al-Khu'i's representative had not been shy about having close contact with Ba'th party officials

> in Samawa and Baghdad. However, his contacts with high-level officials in the presidential palace did not save him. Al-Khu'i and those in his marja'iya didn't protest.

Contrast this with a statement made by an associate of al-Khu'i who was in Najaf at the time. He said that there was no uprising.

> The ulama [who were his followers] deserted Baqir al-Sadr. Those who had been affiliated with him left Iraq about six months before he died. Had they stayed with him, perhaps Saddam would have negotiated with him rather than just taking him away and killing him. No one stood up in protest. No one said anything because no one was there.

The disagreements even over what might be considered straightforward historical facts concerning Baqir al-Sadr's life underscore some basic problems. First, they indicate that there is no consensus whatsoever about the political role a marja' should have. Second, they show that the marja'iya does not have a way to deal with an up-and-coming figure in the system during the lifetime of a major marja'. While al-Khu'i was alive, al-Sadr could not directly put himself forward as a marja', nor could he really find another legitimate (or at least formal) role for himself in the system. He needed to wait until al-Khu'i died, but it is extremely difficult for a person, especially an intellectually energetic one such al-Sadr, to put his life on hold. Third, there exists no objective, relatively unbiased source in which events could be investigated and recorded in a place such as Najaf. Everything would be by word of mouth, subject to faulty memories and the accounts of biased observers.

Building al-Sadr's Marja'iya

A critical time in the life of Baqir al-Sadr came with the sudden death of Muhsin al-Hakim in 1970. Though al-Khu'i was the "ustadh al-hawza" (the professor of the hawza), in Najaf, a title he was given because al-Hakim was preoccupied with other matters and did not teach as much as al-Khu'i, al-Hakim was recognized as the senior 'alim in Iraq. Up until his death, he was looked upon as the grand marja' in Najaf. Al-Hakim's death also precipitated political scrambling by both the Iranian and the Iraqi governments. On the one hand, the new Iraqi Ba'thist regime, which al-Hakim had been plotting to overthrow, wanted a more cooperative jurist to head the Shi'a of Iraq. The Ba'thist regime launched a public campaign supporting their candidate, Shaykh 'Ali Kashif al-Ghita'. Kashif al-Ghita', a member of a well-known religious family and the son of a renowned politically active jurist, was at least not publicly critical of the regime. However, a supporter of the Ba'thists would not be viewed favorably among the members of the hawza, who had not forgotten the ill treatment meted out to al-Hakim by the government. Seeing that their attempts to promote Kashif al-Ghita' were futile, the government then began to expel non-Iraqi students in the hawza to reduce the influence of the religious establishment there.

For its part, the Iranian government also had its own agenda with regard to the marja'iya. As mentioned in the previous chapter, the Shah found it preferable to keep the institution outside of Iran as it was during the time of al-Hakim . Since the death of Borujirdi, the Shah had suffered increasing threats from religious leaders, particularly from Khomeini. With no one of the stature of Borujirdi to fill his role, the Shi'a of Iran largely turned to al-Hakim for leadership. Since al-Hakim was recognized as an Arab and was concerned with Iraqi political matters, the Shah did not feel threatened. However, at the time of the death of al-Hakim, Khomeini was residing in Najaf. Since Khomeini's focus was Iran, the prospect of having him recognized as the grand marja' while outside the control of the Iranian government was not pleasant to contemplate for the Shah.

As it happened, the person who was actually the most conspicuous candidate in religious terms for the marja'iya also turned out to be an acceptable candidate to both the Iranians and the Iraqis. Iraq was satisfied that al-Khu'i was Iranian and not concerned with Iraqi matters. The Iranian government was happy to have an apolitical Iranian who was outside of Iran and who—it was hoped—could silence protest in the hawza of Qom. They wanted him to be a counterweight to Khomeini with whom he did not have a cordial relationship. Al-Khu'i's prestige by the time of the death of al-Hakim was well established. In order to hedge its bets, the Iranian government also promoted the marja'iya of other jurists, such as Shari'atmadari.

By this time al-Khu'i had taught in the hawza for more than four decades, and hundreds of jurists claimed to be his students. In fact, one could not find a jurist that had studied in the hawza of Najaf who did not claim to have attended al-Khu'i seminars in fiqh and usul. As we have seen earlier, there is tremendous advantage in having so many high-ranking jurists all over the Shi'i world advocating for one as a marja'. Yet, in spite of al-Khu'i's stature in the hawza, he still faced challenges to his leadership. The al-Hakim family, building on their father's legacy, wanted the marja'iya to remain "in the household." The Hakims campaigned for al-Hakim's eldest son, Yusuf, to fill the role vacated by his father. In his sixties at the time of the senior al-Hakim's death, he was already a well-known jurist with large audiences and many advocates, though he lacked al-Khu'i's reputation in the fields of fiqh and usual. Yusuf al-Hakim tried garnering support by increasing the salaries of his students in the hawza, a common practice in such instances. Ultimately, though, he could not truly compete with very learned al-Khu'i and had to concede the position and to advise others to follow the senior teacher.

Khomeini too was a contender, but he was no match for the popularity and educational credentials of al-Khu'i. Arab students complained that he taught classes in Persian. Having smaller classes in the hawza than al-Khu'i, he also had fewer followers. Moreover, the fact that Khomeini's associates had access to Iraqi radio transmissions to Iran, and thus were presumably cooperating with the Ba'thist regime, led to chilly feelings towards him on the part of Iraqi Shi'i activists.

None of these possible options for the marja'iya seems to have satisfied the al-Da'wa people. Headed by Sahib Dakhil, a top leader of the Da'wa Party, they approached the former grand jurist of the movement, Baqir al-Sadr, to pledge their allegiance to him and offer their support for his marja'iya. However, al-Sadr knew that his quest for the marja'iya had slim prospects. Al-Sadr himself referred to al-Khu'i as "ustadhi," (my teacher), and it is a well-respected principle that one cannot openly seek the marja'iya while one's his teacher is still in the hawza. With Baqir al-Sadr refusing to challenge al-Khu'i directly, the al-Da'wa leadership then approached Khomeini to offer their support to him as the marja', yet he too reportedly refused, saying that they needed to turn to the "professor of the hawza," al-Khu'i. Reluctantly, they turned to al-Khu'i, but having sought their leadership elsewhere first, they reportedly were rebuffed by al-Khu'i's representatives in the hawza and were told that al-Khu'i did not need their endorsement.

Al-Sadr's Teaching in Najaf

> The pedagogical ideal of the madrasa is just the reverse [of the secular system]. . . There are no grades, so students study only for learning's sake. Students who do not study are not flunked out, but neither are they elevated by bribery or favoritism. For each there is a place according to his capacity and inclination: a village preacher (akhund) need not be legal expert (mujtahid). Students study with teachers of their own choice. There is thus never a disciplinary problem or a problem of lack of respect for teachers. Indeed the bond of respect and devotion of students for their teachers is proverbial. . . Teachers do not pontificate; rather, all teaching is on a dialectic principle of argument and counterargument in which students are encouraged to participate insofar as they have the preparation to do so.[65]

But was Baqir al-Sadr really out of the running for the marja'iya? It is in the nature of the marja'iya that there is ambiguity, and this ambiguity

[65] Fischer, *Iran,* pp. 61-63.

enables people other than the most notable jurist to rise to high levels of prominence in the community. Yet rising to prominence while such a senior mujtahid as al-Khu'i was alive is a delicate business. While he found it highly undesirable to jeopardize his relationship with al-Khu'i, al-Sadr also wished to establish himself in the running for the marja'iya. To do so would involve taking gradual, yet calculated steps, principally by advancing his academic credentials. Al-Sadr started conducting regular seminars in bahth al-kharij in usul and fiqh as well as publishing works that would prove his authority in these disciplines.

Once again, whether or not a supporter of Baqir al-Sadr is speaking determines the picture one gleans about his efforts. According to Shaykh Nasiri, al-Sadr's older brother Isma'il started attending his younger brother's bahth al-kharij classess because Baqir surpassed Isma'il in his knowledge of fiqh and usul. Some sources even report that that al-Khu'i said he had "never encountered a deeper approach to investigating those disciplines than that of al-Sadr." Talib al-Rifa'i, one of the founders of al-Da'wa, relates that, emplying the Socratic method of teaching used in the hawza, Baqir al-Sadr countered a thesis proposed by al-Khu'i on a particular issue. This was followed with an argument from al-Khu'i. According to al-Rifa'i, this round of exchanges continued through nine sessions until al-Khu'i yielded to al-Sadr's final thesis. Yet not all religious Shi'a would have spoken about al-Sadr's role in this exchange in such glowing terms.

Sadr's seminars in bahth al-kharij began in the early 1970s. They followed the classic method of teaching. His fiqh seminars consisted of commentaries on and arguments about of the century-old legal manual of Kazim al-Yazdi (d. 1918), known as *al-'Urwa al-Wuthqa*. This book has been reprinted numerous times in order to add more recent opinions of prominent scholars to the original work and to previous commentaries. Al-Sadr, in true traditional form, would cite arguments from earlier jurists who had tackled the particular legal issue at hand and provide counter-arguments and various legal views on each fatwa. In fact, the entire religious teaching method consisted of commentaries upon commentaries. Students would write notes upon notes of their teachers' lectures. While al-Sadr questioned the utility of this approach, obviously he felt compelled to use it if he wanted to be considered for the role of marja'.

But if he were to attain the marja'iya these considerations had to be, at least for the time being, put aside. To be seen as the heir apparent of al-Khu'i, he had to prove his authority in the classical methods of teaching and writing in fiqh and usul. His previous scholarship, including his works in economics and philosophy, would bring him no credit in the hawza. His was a struggle to satisfy the requirements of the traditions of the hawza, without which he could never attain the position he sought, while at the same time bringing about the innovations he sought to strengthen the institution he aspired to.

In fact, Baqir al-Sadr's innovations went beyond the hawza and its teaching methods. Such internal innovations in themselves would have been enough to put him at odds with the establishment. However, other changes he sought would prove to be even more controversial as they would, if implemented, eventually undermine the entire structure of the ulama.[66] At the heart of his message was the implication that the dividing line between ulama and layman should no longer be clearly drawn. In advocating that mujtahids write their treatises in a jargon-free style, easily accessible to the muqallid, he was essentially saying that mediators between the mujtahid and the muqallid would be unnecessary. His argument was that the classical style of writing in the hawza—in particular, the risala as a manual of law for laymen—could be justified when most of the people were illiterate. However, with the advancement of education, the laymen should be able to pick up the writings of the mujtahid and comprehend his writings on his or her own. Since the majority of al-Sadr's followers were Islamic activists and either college students or professionals, he addressed his own writings to this audience. In his writings juristic terminology is simplified. In producing *al-Fatawa al-Wadiha* (The clear rulings), his own manual of law, his goal was to make a text as simple as possible so that it could be comprehended by the general public. With the editorial help of a Lebanese shaykh, Muhammad-Jawad Mughniya, he produced a legal text that gained significant popularity.

Sadr also sought to change the taxonomy for legal codes, thereby again breaking with the age-old traditions of the hawza. Rather than having merely two categories of legal texts, ʻibadat (acts of worship) and muʻamalat (transactions), al-Sadr proposed new categories that divided up the legal system so that public and private matters could be addressed differently.[67] In the classical system, as outlined in *al-'Urwa al-Wuthqa* of Ayatollah Kazim Yazdi (d. 1918), family matters were discussed in the section on transactions, since marriage was considered as a mere contract between a man and a women. Even stranger, Yazdi discusses governance in section on buying and selling, since it deals with the legal authority for sales transactions. To overcome such discrepancies and to give Islamic law a modern flavor, Sadr suggested that family matters must to be

---

[66] "Baqir al-Sadr's Quest for the Marjaʻiya. In Linda S. Walbridge, ed., *The Most Learned of the Shiʻah: The Institution of the* Marjaʻ Taqlīd (New York: Oxford, 2001), p. 140–48.
[67] Aziz, "Quest."

placed in a separate category with financial transcations and contracts in another. The last chapter, Sadr suggests, should deal with public matters, such as Islamic gorvenment, the scope of its authority, the role of the judiciary, religious taxes (zakat and khums), and the issue of war and social conflict (jihad and the 'promotion of virtue and prevention of vice').

Sadr's departure with tradition and the perception that he was addressing the concerns of modern, educated Shi'a generated enthusiasm among the new breed of Islamists. Particularly when speaking with Shi'a raised and educated in Baghdad, one senses the impact he had on people's lives. Men and women have both said that before they became familiar with the ideas of Baqir al-Sadr they paid no attention to religion. Baqir al-Sadr's younger sister, known as Bint al-Huda (Daughter of Guidance), helped spread of his fame among women. Encouraging women to follow the precepts of Islam while encouraging both religious and secular education and involvement in worldly matters had enormous appeal for Shi'i women who, feeling distant from the way of life of Najaf and Karbala, had few means of expressing their latent religious feelings. Bint al-Huda and her brother presented a model of a new type of religiosity. Baqir al-Sadr's students, some from abroad, began advancing his ideas and his marja'iya. They urged him to write a risala of his own. Again, he found himself faced with the dilemma of wishing to put himself forward without jeopardizing his relationship with al-Khu'i. His solution was to record his opinions as footnotes to Muhsin al-Hakim's risala, *Minhaj al-Salihin,* hoping thereby to ward off criticism by al-Khu'i's followers while still advancing his own ideas and his legalistic capabilities.

This approach did not mollify al-Khu'i's entourage. Rumors began to circulate around the hawza that al-Khu'i was dissatisfied with al-Sadr. In response, al-Sadr paid a visit to al-Khu'i in an effort to smooth relations with him. Such a visit would in and of itself indicate that Baqir al-Sadr did not see himself on a level with the senior jurist. As further proof that he was not challenging al-Khu'i's authority, al-Sadr asked one of his companions to write a letter addressed to him seeking his opinion about the marja'iya. Al-Sadr then replied to the letter, directing the people to follow the guidance of Ayatollah al-Khu'i. In addition, al-Sadr continued to keep in close contact with al-Khu'i, paying him a visit every time he had a juristic opinion differing from al-Khu'i's and seeking his approval. He also asked his closest associates not to publicly promote his marja'iya, but rather to propagate it discretely and only to those few who believed in his authority in fiqh. As a result, his muqallids mostly consisted of intellectuals, college students, and members of the upper middle class. They were mainly Iraqis and tended to be religious activists and al-Da'wa members. It is instructive that even his beloved sister, Bint al-Huda, devoted as she was to her brother, was not muqallid to him. She followed al-Khu'i.

Al-Sadr's efforts to defuse the conflict between him and the office of Ayatollah al-Khu'i were mostly in vain. His writings and opinions testified to his quest for the marja'iya, and there was no question that his reputation was spreading. Al-Khu'i's associates saw him as an upstart or worse, undermining the grand marja'. Supporters of al-Sadr say that his students and close associates were the targets of character assassinations in the hawza and that the teachers in the hawza were reluctant even to use al-Sadr's textbook on jurisprudence, *Durus fi 'Ilm al-Usul*. Muhammad al-Husayni has written that one teacher, Shaykh Hadi al-Radi, used to hide in the basement of a school in Najaf in order to teach al-Sadr's text on usul, known as *Halaqat* (Seminars). Al-Sadr himself was even reported to have been the target of harassment in Najaf. Al-Husayni tells that al-Sadr attended a funeral where the people present would not make a place for him to sit inside the hall. He was forced to sit by the door where people removed their shoes.

In protest, al-Sadr cancelled his lectures in fiqh and usul in 1978. Only with mediation between al-Khu'i and al-Sadr and the encouragement from his friend, Shaykh Muhammad Jawad Mughniya, did he finally resume his courses there. However, al-Sadr's public protest was considered quite out of the ordinary, and relations between al-Sadr and al-Khu'i remained as strained as ever. Al-Husayni states that at this point al-Khu'i began to indicate that one Nasrullah al-Mustanbit might be a likely successor to the marja'iya.

Apparently, relations between the two men never healed, though there are differing accounts of this story. Supporters of al-Sadr say that even the government's crackdown on al-Sadr and al-Da'wa did not bring about reconciliation between al-Sadr and al-Khu'i and his associates. They claim that even during al-Sadr's nine months of detention, Ayatollah al-Khu'i never paid a visit, nor did he issue any statement in support of al-Sadr. They contend that the indifference shown to his wellbeing played a pivotal role in signaling to the Ba'thist government that al-Sadr was isolated and that there would be no protest should he be executed.

Ayatollah al-Khu'i's son, Sayyid Majid al-Khu'i, gives an altogether different account. According to him, al-Khu'i asked Baqir al-Sadr several times not to be involved in politics.

> Baqir al-Sadr came to see my father [Ayatollah al-Khu'i] after his first arrest in Baghdad. Through his son Jamal, my father expressed concern for his wellbeing and told him that if he would refrain from political activity, he could protect him.

Majid al-Khu'i quotes his father as saying directly to Baqir al-Sadr on one occasion, "Please, just do your religious job." But Baqir al-Sadr reportedly replied, "Everything is finished." Al-Khu'i said, "If you sit here with me, they won't touch you." But Baqir al-Sadr refused. Sayyid Majid adds, "We lost Baqir al-Sadr for nothing. My father had a long, normal life, and he did whatever he could do. Baqir al-Sadr died without having done his work."[68]

Reforming the Marja'iya

Baqir al-Sadr is particularly interesting in the context of this book because of his endeavors to completely overhaul the institution of the marja'iya. The marja'iya was the one institution that the Shi'a had developed that had the potential to organize the community politically as well as religiously. Yet, it still lacked institutional underpinnings. In particular, Baqir al-Sadr was concerned that there was no means to enforce the opinions of a marja'. He could not even make his appointed representatives, let alone the laymen who were muqallid to him, heed his wishes and obey his decisions.

In Chapter Two, we outlined what al-Sadr considered the four historical stages of the marja'iya. While changes in the marja'iya have occurred overtime, al-Sadr says that the one thing that has remained constant was that the marja' has always conducted his policies and made his decisions on the basis of his own individual style. Each marja' has depended on an inner circle of close associates and family members to gather information, issue statements, and make decisions. Thus, al-Sadr says, there were no fundamental patterns either for the process of making decisions or for the content of those decisions. This situation invited inconsistencies that resulted in social confusion, ultimately weakening the relations between the marja' and the people. The lack of an institutional structure also meant that, once a marja' died, there was no bureaucracy in place to carry on the duties of the office. Each marja' started with his own retinue, and each marja' had to start from square one to conduct his business. This lack of structure and clearly defined roles meant that the significance of the personality and leadership style of the marja' was accentuated.

In his writings al-Sadr makes it clear that he wished to see the power of the marja'iya enhanced. This, he believed, could be done by transforming what he called the "individualistic marja'iya" into an "institutional marja'iya"—that is, rather than having a person rising to this

[68] JW: It is ironic then that Majid al-Khu'i himself died while attempting to intervene in the chaotic politics of the 2003 American invasion of Iraq; see John and Linda Walbridge, "Son of an Ayatollah," in Trix et al, *Muslim Voices*, pp. 43–55.

status through a vague process and be surrounded by an entourage of relatives and close associates, there needs to be a full-fledged institution. He wished to see committees of experts in different fields give advice to the marja' and execute his decisions. Institutionalizing the marja'iya, he believed, would prevent the jurist from making arbitrary decisions and would also serve to train new jurists. The power of the jurist should, in al-Sadr's view, be checked by free competition for the position of marja'. The jurist must be able to demonstrate his intellectual and spiritual qualities to the public, thereby making it possible for the people to elect their marja' from among various candidates. The administrative duties and the main political power should be vested in the people. Al-Sadr's writings suggest that he believed that, during the Occultation of the Twelfth Imam, the people are virtually in the position of God in the election their leaders.

In assessing al-Sadr's view of the marja'iya, it is apparent that he visualized it in terms very much like that of the papacy. While the pope is the vicar of Christ, who in Catholic belief is God, the marja' also serves as a divine representative, though in a slightly less direct manner. According to al-Sadr, God established the role of "shahid" (witness). The shahid is the one who would take responsibility for conveying divine guidance to mankind. Prophets were the first to be assigned this role. Since the prophet cannot be a constant presence, others need to succeed him in his role as shahid, namely the Imams. In the absence of the Imams, the scholars of religious law—which is to say, the maraji'—act in the role of shahid. In al-Sadr's words,

> The shahid, from an ideological perspective, is the authority on belief and legislation who oversees the social journey and its congruence, ideologically, with the divine message. He is also responsible for getting the [human] journey back on its right course in case of any deviation that might occur during the application [of the message]. The marja', as the successor of the prophets and the Imams, must possess the qualifications—i.e., 'ilm (knowledge) and 'adl (justice). However, unlike prophethood and imamate, the marja'iya is not divinely ordained and specially chosen by God. It is not the person, per se, who is of great importance; it is his qualifications. In other words, the marja' is the legitimate successor of the prophet and Imams and thus is the shahid by virtue of his qualifications.[69]

However, al-Sadr believed that these two qualifications, while necessary, are not sufficient for the leadership of the umma. The marja' must understand social conditions and how these conditions affect religion. He proposed a "social foundation" that would make the impact of the marja'

[69] Talib Aziz "Political Theory," pp. 59-60.

in social affairs more effective and of longer duration than the lifespan of a single marja'. His prescription for the problem was to establish an institution in which the marja' himself is the center and where its structure, role, and process are thoroughly defined. While he presents further particulars of the changes that he found desirable, the core of his argument is that the marja'iya will be ineffective so long as its traditional form survives. Formalization, centralization, and continuity are key concepts to its reform. Implicit in his writings is his desire to rid the institution of the role that kinsmen automatically inherit in the running of the marja'iya. In his words, the offices of the marja' will "replace the court which represents an arbitrary individualistic structure made up of individuals grouped by chance who fulfill some immediate needs but exhibit a superficial mentality without any defined and clear objective."[70]

Baqir al-Sadr's ideas did not die with him. The popularity of his ideas and writings are probably on the level of those of the Iranian Shi'ite ideologue, 'Ali Shari'ati. In personal interviews I have found that Sunnis, particularly of the younger, educated generation who are interested in having Islam address the challenges of the modern world, refer to the works of Baqir al-Sadr. Chibli Mallat has shown how his ideas have been put into effect in the Islamic Republic of Iran.[71] Perhaps most interesting, though, is the manner in which Baqir al-Sadr's ideas have been carried on by Shaykh Muhammad Husayn Fadlallah of Lebanon, who is the subject of the next chapter.

---

70 Talib Aziz "Political Theory," p. 58.

71 Mallat, *Renewal*, pp. 59–110.

Chapter 6

Imam Fadlallah of Lebanon

SAYYID, COMMONLY CALLED "Shaykh," Muhammad Husayn Fadlallah, one of ten children, was born in Najaf in 1935 to a religious family from Lebanon. He was a descendant of Imam Hasan and was the nephew of Ayatollah Muhsin al-Hakim's fourth wife, a member of the huge Bezzi family of south Lebanon and the mother of Ayatollah al-Hakim's most notable children: Mahdi, Muhammad Baqir, and 'Abdu'l-Aziz. Fadlallah's education began in what is called "al-Katatib," seminary classes designed to teach the alphabet and the Qur'an. In a book by 'Ali Hasan Sarur, entitled *Fadlallah wa-Tahaddi al-Mamnu'* (Fadlallah and the Challenge of the Impossible),[72] Fadlallah is reported to have recalled the harshness of the discipline he and his classmates received at the hands of their teachers in al-Katatib. The falaqa, the punishment in which a student would have his feet tied and the soles of his feet beaten, was employed whenever a student made a simple mistake. He later enrolled in Muntada al-Nashir, a newly formed Islamic school that was similar to governmental school in Iraq.

Najaf for Fadlallah was both a training ground in the classical religious subjects of fiqh and usul and also a place where he was introduced to the writings of Najaf's many poets. At ten, he produced a handwritten newsletter entitled, *al-Adab* with the cooperation of his cousin, Mahdi al-Hakim. Fadlallah would read Egyptian literary magazines such as *al-Katib* and started writing poetry himself when only a child. At the age of twelve, he delivered his own poem in a public gathering for the occasion

72 'A. Ḥ. Sarūr, *Faḍl Allāh wa-Taḥaddī al-Mamnū'* ([Lebanon]: Tawzī' al-Sharika al-'Āmmah li'l-Khadamāt al-Inmā'īya, 1992).

of the Arabs' loss of Palestine. This was the same year he joined the hawza and started his religious studies. Fadlallah's love of poetry was not deemed commendable by the Najafi establishment. Poetry was not generally seen as a fit endeavor for the ulama of Najaf, yet his uncle, Muhammad Sa'id Fadlallah and Ayatollah Hadi al-Shirazi, recognized as a marja' taqlid in Karbala, both encouraged Fadlallah's love of poetry. Hadi Shirazi reputedly was himself a poet and shared some of his poetry with Fadlallah. One could say that Fadlallah was influenced by the extremes of Najaf society and its environs. A student of both al-Hakim and al-Khu'i, he was part of the religious establishment with its shrines and seminaries, but he was also a part of the flourishing secularism of the youthful intelligentsia of Najaf. He seems to have been as comfortable with the rather dry studies of fiqh and usul as he was with the more literary and romantic world of poetry.

There continued to be many contradictions in Shaykh Fadlallah's life. He was a close friend of his contemporary Baqir al-Sadr, while he was also a representative of both al-Khu'i and Khomeini during their lifetimes. A student of al-Khu'i, he spoke out in favor of the theory of wilayat al-faqih, advocated by Khomeini and discredited by al-Khu'i. With the formation of Jama'at al-'Ulama and al-Da'wa in the aftermath of the 1958 revolution, Fadlallah was recruited by al-Sadr to write the second editorial of *al-Adwa'*, entitled "Kalimatuna" (Our Opinion). He later took over as editor of the journal when al-Sadr resigned. Considered by those who knew him as one of the main theoreticians and apologists of al-Da'wa, he was depended upon by Lebanon's Hezbollah—which is at odds with al-Da'wa—for their legitimacy, yet he was popular in the Christian press in Lebanon, and his Friday sermons were broadcast on television. It is not unusual to see a picture of Fadlallah on a billboard for Christian television, announcing a live interview with him! A supporter of Gulpaygani in Qom as grand marja' after the deaths of al-Khu'i and Khomeini, he incurred the anger of the Iranian government for not supporting their candidate, Araki. However, he subjected himself to Gulpayagani's public disapproval because of his very liberal views, particularly concerning Sunni/Shi'i relations. A jurist who is famous among the Shi'i community for his feminist views and who has declared everyone tahir (ritually pure), he had a reputation in the United States as the archetypal narrowminded religious fanatic who wished to destroy America and everything it stands for.

One might very well ask, who is this man? The one thing that it might be safe to say is that he is probably the most controversial and enigmatic faqih in the Shi'i world. A look at some of his concerns and rulings may show why he enjoys the adulation of some and the wrath of others, while leaving the remainder in some confusion. One of the most controversial subjects he embarked upon was that of the legality of masturbation for women. Although it cannot be said that Fadlallah condones this practice, he has challenged the rationale other jurists have used in debating this issue. The prohibition against female masturbation has been based on the idea that women have a semen-like fluid, similar to that of men. Since the ejaculation of this fluid is only permissible during intercourse, masturbation has been forbidden for both sexes. Fadlallah consulted physicians and scientists at the American University of Beirut and, based on the information he gathered, concluded that women do not have such a fluid. Since the reasoning behind the prohibition against female masturbation was faulty, the prohibition could not stand. Fadlallah went on to say that he does not condone women's masturbation because he believes it is psychologically detrimental. While his defenders say that he ultimately forbids the practice, other ulama accuse him of allowing it. He, for his part, challenges these ulama and his students to question "antiquated" reasoning and not confine themselves to the traditions of previous jurists.[73] The question of where he comes down in this position has not been settled, as there are Shi'a who admire Fadlallah, but who have distanced themselves from him because of the manner in which he approached this topic.

Other rulings also fly in the face of those of the conservative ulama. According to Fadlallah playing games similar to gambling is permitted if no money is involved. Unlike other jurists, he allows the shaving of the beard. His most progressive fatwa deals with the issue of ritual purity. While some modern jurists, most notably the late Muhsin al-Hakim and Muhammad-Baqir al-Sadr, held that the "people of the book" (ahl al-kitab) are ritually pure, Fadlallah's takes this issue a step further. He considers all people in general to be tahir regardless of their religious affiliation.

In this ruling we seem to find a key to at least a part of Fadlallah's ideology. Fadlallah's rulings often lead in the direction of breaking down barriers between the Shi'a and other groups—whether they be other Muslims or non-Muslims. In the process he often finds himself attacking some of the basic concepts that have constituted a unique Shi'i identity and coming to loggerheads with many of his peers and rank-and-file Shi'a. His ruling that it is allowable to depend on astronomical calculations or to use modern techniques for the sighting of the moon means that Shi'a would be celebrating religious holidays in conjunction with Sunnis, not a day or two later as they have often done. The Shi'a have traditionally believed that maghrib (sunset) prayers should begin at dark-

[73] *al-Minhaj al-Istidlali,* reference not traced.

ness, not at sunset per se. Fadlallah disagrees. "Sunset" means sunset, as far as he is concerned. Such rulings have major repercussions. Postponing prayers until later than those of the Sunnis was a reminder to the Shi'a of their distinctiveness. If all Muslims prayed at the same time, this reminder would vanish. Public displays during Muharram, invoking the name of Imam 'Ali in the adhan—practices very much at the core of traditional Shi'i ritual life—are as questionable and not essential to Shi'i rituals in Fadlallah's eyes. In a 1992 sermon Fadlallah declared as untrue the story that accuses the first two caliphs, Abu Bakr and 'Umar, of violently crushing the Prophet's daughter Fatima and causing the loss of her unborn baby.

Not surprisingly, Fadlallah found that he had to defend himself, particularly to Gulpaygani and the other ulama in Qom, who found his views out of line with Shi'i thought.

The Feminist Fadlallah

During the Fourth Annual Conference of the Muslim Group of the USA and Canada (See chapter eight for a discussion of this group), held in St. Louis, Missouri, during the Christmas vacation in December, 1982, Fadlallah was among the speakers. During the question and answer period, some of the men expressed their concern that his views would "corrupt their wives" and asked him not to voice them.[74]

Fadlallah's opinions about women are often at odds with those of other jurists. While Islamic "fundamentalism" is usually linked in people's minds with a more restricted role for women and conjures up images of the female as a totally covered shapeless form, Fadlallah insists that only modesty is required. He does not elaborate on whether the wrist bone needs to be covered or the chin or every strand of hair. The obsession with female modesty that held in the Islamic Republic of Iran, especially in the early days of the revolution, was not his concerns.

Instead he addresses the actual role that women have in the family and society. The only one of her responsibilities in marriage that is dictated by religion, he says, is that she satisfy her husband's sexual desires. Other than that, he argues, she is free to practice her "natural social, political, and economic duties and rights."[75] While other jurists have written that women do not have to breastfeed their children, nor should they be compelled to keep house without an allowance, it is Fadlallah who

---

[74] During this visit to the United States, some of his student hosts dressed him in Western clothes and took him on the public tour of the White House.

[75] As cited in his *Min Waḥy al-Qur'ān* (3rd ed.; Beirut: Dār al-Zahrā', 1985) and *Ta'ammulāt Islāmīya ḥawla al-Mar'ah* ([Beirut] : Dār al-Malāk, 1992).

emphasizes these points. However, he does not completely dismiss these as outside of women's domain. Rather, he says that the wife should perform tasks in the home out of a sense of love, not due to coercion. In other words, he appears to envision a more or less traditional division of family labor but in a family whose members perform their tasks out of a desire to create a harmonious relationship. During sermons, he has stated that a husband cannot deny his wife the right to leave her husband's house to attend religious gatherings, so long as she has fulfilled her marital duties—that is, satisfied her husband's sexual needs. Fadlallah has expressed the view that the traditional Muslim marriage, as advocated by traditional jurists, is like a prison for women. He has mused aloud that he wonders why women marry at all if they are faced with such inhumane treatment from their husbands.

Fadlallah does not state that his liberal position on women is due to the exigencies of the day or the needs of the Shi'a who now reside in the West. Rather, he says that his opinions are purely derived from Islamic law. He is critical of the fact that Islamic principles have traditionally been molded to satisfy cultural belief or to conform to political pressure. Contemporary jurists then follow in the footsteps of their predecessors rather than taking a fresh look at the law itself. He objects to the writings of former jurists as having been elevated to sacred scripture.

Fadlallah and the Modernist Movements

His peers may look upon Fadlallah as a renegade, but there is something of the modern day religious hero about one who is viewed as being at the forefront of the struggle against Israeli and Western forces. Here we see Fadlallah's mastery as the religious scholar/politician.

When Fadlallah finished his religious studies, he left for Lebanon in 1966 and resided in al-Naba'a, a western suburb of Beirut where there is a small Shi'i community. When there, he founded "Usrat al-Ta'akhi," which included a clinic and a women's organization. He formed a mini-hawza to teach young Lebanese ulama and preached in his parents' hometown in southern Lebanon. He published his collection of seminars in a series of pamphlets in which he outlines his views, which are considered "modernist" by his admirers.

As for his relations with the famous Musa al-Sadr, cousin of the Imam Baqir al-Sadr, he mostly avoided conflict with him. He was against the formation of the Shi'i Council formed by Musa al-Sadr in 1969 on the grounds that it would divide the Muslims in Lebanon and intensify sectarian divisions in the country. However, he did encourage the formation of Amal in 1975 as a means to recruit Shi'i youth who were increasingly drawn to the leftist organizations. The paramilitary and political nature of Amal, he hoped, would be a way of drawing them back to religion. Throughout the Lebanese civil war, he remained active, strengthening his contacts with the local population, attending conferences, providing social services to war victims, and keeping in touch with the religious establishment and the marja'iya. Though residing in Lebanon, far from the centers of Shi'ism, he managed to never become marginalized. In fact, with the rise of the Khomeini to power in Iran, Fadlallah's students, his sermons and his writings became central to the process of Islamizing the government in Iran.

Through the entire process, however, it has not been easy to pin Fadlallah down and clearly define him. Depending on whom one speaks to, he is considered the spiritual leader of Hezbollah, the defender of the traditional marja'iya of al-Khu'i, the jurist with close political ties to an assortment of unsavory regimes (Syria, Algeria, Saudi Arabia), while also being the political mobilizer of the masses. He was probably the only jurist invited to an official Iranian conference capable of delivering a speech in the hawza of Qom in defense of al-Khu'i without jeopardizing his status with the Khomeini clique.

Although the Hezbollah fighters follow their sponsor in Tehran, Fadlallah was still perceived as being at the front line of this "jihad." He managed a delicate balance so as not to antagonize too greatly either the Iranians or the Syrians. Ideologically at odds in many respects with Hezbollah, he kept close working relations with their leadership. Since its opposition in Lebanon tends to label Hezbollah as an agent of a foreign country, it has needed legitimacy of a local nature. The charismatic Fadlallah, by sanctioning its activities, provided this legitimacy. For example, during the 1980s when Hezbollah was at war with Harakat Amal, Hezbollah could have been perceived as being agents of their foreign sponsor, Iran, fighting against their Shi'i Lebanese brothers. Fadlallah issued a fatwa saying that Hezbollah was justly defending itself against Amal, thus saving Hezbollah from political annihilation.

Amal has had its own religious figurehead, Shaykh Muhammad Mahdi Shams al-Din. During the fifties and early sixties, both Fadlallah and Shams al-Din were part of the growing movement in Najaf to politicize Islam. Both men were recruited by al-Sadr to write for the journal *al-Adwa'*. Fadlallah in a private interview credits al-Sadr's encouragement in this endeavor as being instrumental in his later success as a writer. When al-Sadr resigned from his position as the editor-in-chief of *al-Adwa'*, Fadlallah took that role and Shams al-Din started contributing to the journal. While neither of the two men appear ever to have been official members of al-Da'wa, they essentially preached the same sort of philosophy as the Najafi al-Da'wa group. Theirs was an intellectual, rationalist approach appealing to the intelligentsia. It conflicted with the Musa al-Sadr/Khomeini emotionalism that aimed to attract and mobilize the masses. As long as Musa al-Sadr was alive, the two men avoided getting into conflict with him. Musa al-Sadr was simply too dominant and imposing a figure to take on. Yet, the two men responded to their rather precarious position vis-à-vis Musa al-Sadr in different ways. Fadlallah opted to distance himself from the Lebanese Shi'i Council while keeping contact with Musa al-Sadr through his cousin, Baqir al-Sadr. Shams al-Din, on the other hand, encouraged by Al-Da'wa supporters, opted to become involved in the Shi'i Council, becoming Musa al-Sadr's deputy.

For twenty years Fadlallah and Shams al-Din worked together, yet in the late 1980's and 1990's, they became the bitterest of enemies. The hostilities between the two men are linked with the divisions between Hezbollah (the Party of God), founded after Israel's 1982 invasion of Lebanon, and the Amal Movement, mentioned above.

During the tumult of the Lebanese civil war, the Iranian Revolution, and the disappearance of Musa al-Sadr, Fadlallah and Shams al-Din were left in the shadows. However, after the 1983 bombing of the Marine barracks in Lebanon, Fadlallah was suddenly portrayed by the Western press as the leader of the suicide attackers, despite his repeated denials. He has also been credited with being the spiritual head of the Hezbollah Movement.

Once again, though, the situation is not nearly so clear as the press would like its readers to think. According to reliable informants, it was the Iranian ambassador to Damascus, Ali-Akbar Muhtashimi who was generally thought to be the mastermind of Hezbollah. He gathered many young revolutionary ulama who were influenced by the Iranian revolution. However, the rank and file of the party in the early period were al-Da'wa members living in Lebanon, religious elements within Harakat Amal, as well as Iranian sympathizers. Many of these were students of Fadlallah in his seminary so that he had an indirect influence in the party, but he could not be said to be its head. Yet his stature rose, especially when it became known that the CIA attempted to kill him in a car bomb that left more than 200 people dead.[76]

With his rise and that of Hezbollah, Shams al-Din's stature was threatened. Aligning himself with Harakat Amal and its leader Nabih Berri, he was then portrayed by Hezbollah as having sold out to a non-religious organization. From the opposing perspective, because Fadlallah was so closely linked in the minds of outsiders with Hezbollah of Leba-

---

[76] Bob Woodard, *Veil: The Secret Wars of the CIA, 1981-1987* (New York: Simon and Schuster, 1987), pp. 396–98.

non, it is assumed that he supported the Iranian, and Hezbollah, view of an ulama-run state. In reality, Fadlallah's ideas on the issue of Islam and the state are more closely in line with those of the al-Da'wa movement where the emphasis is on the role of the party, which leads the struggle and seizes the state. In the Hezbollah model, it is the wali-faqih who does so. Hezbollah sees the al-Da'wa model as a Western, foreign ideology, an ideology that is referred to as "backwards" by some because it hinders the spread of the "line of the Imam" (i.e., Khomeini). There were attempts by the ulama to disguise the ill feelings between the two men, but with Shams al-Din openly speaking out against Fadlallah on a tour of the United States, it became impossible to disguise the problems any longer.

In spite of their common backgrounds and the desperate need in Lebanon to unite the Shi'i people, if not all of the Lebanese, these two men were unable to settle their disputes. Perhaps it is Shi'i idealism itself that makes compromise in such situations so difficult. Each is committed to the basic premise that he is rightly guided. Under such circumstances, conceding one's position at all is to admit remoteness from the path of God. The rift between the two men had serious consequences for the Shi'i community at large. Shams al-Din's role as the official representative for Ayatollah Sistani gave him leverage to undermine the reputation of Fadlallah, which he was known to do both in public and private forums. Because Fadlallah gained his own following as a religious leader, Shams al-Din's attacks on him could have had the ultimate result of actually undermining Sistani as the marja'.

Fadlallah is also well accustomed to attacks that extend beyond the borders of Lebanon. For example, in 1996 Fadil al-Maliki, an Iraqi 'alim and a protégé of Muhammad-Baqir al-Hakim, spoke disparagingly of Fadlallah during a sermon commemorating the martyrdom of the Imam Husayn. Members of the audience who were close to Fadlallah were enraged by his comments and launched a public campaign to boycott al-Maliki's sermons. Defenders of al-Maliki said that Fadlallah had demonized others for years and deserved such criticism.

The fact that other Shi'a would publicly condemn a renowned jurist is telling. Disagreements among high-ranking ulama—and even lower ranking ones—are usually not played out in such a visible way. But Fadlallah was exceptional in many respects. It was not just his views on women and non-Shi'a that had the potential of making him so unpopular. Rather, it appears to be the fact that he wished to reform the entire system of Shi'i leadership, so that both the traditional and the radical ulama find his views threatening.

Fadlallah does not shy away from countering his detractors. He has attacked the credibility of those ulama whom he argues have no credentials in religious studies and are not qualified to lead the people. He claimed that he witnessed the graduation of ulama in post-revolutionary Iran where students in the hawza take "crash courses" long on political propaganda and short on religious education.[77] He complained that these poorly educated ulama have flooded the religious seminaries and now control the mosques. He advocated for rigorous legal studies and thorough examinations before a person can become a preacher or jurist. His ideas were put forth in two books *Khutuwat 'ala Tariq al-Islam* (Steps in the path of Islam) and *Qadayana 'ala Daw' al-Islam* (Our judgments in the light of Islam), which were standard readings for Shi'i (and other Muslim) activists in the sixties and seventies—before Khomeinism became the predominant mode.[78]

However, he has not limited himself to verbal counterattacks. Fadlallah, according to his admirers, was a paragon of self-discipline who lectured every Friday in his Beirut mosque and had a regular schedule for reading and writing, which is extremely important for the jurist. His "mini-hawza" in Damascus indoctrinateed and trained young Islamists and provided social, religious, and family services to the community. His Jam'iyat al-Mabarrat al-Khayriya, a foundation for housing, feeding, and educating hundreds of orphans in war-ravaged Lebanon, has certainly put him in good stead with many of the people in Lebanon. He was able to provide funding for these projects himself as he was authorized to collect khums for both al-Khu'i and Khomeini during their lifetimes. In fact, the orphanage was first started with a single project funded by Ayatollah al-Khu'i in the early eighties, and was called "Mabarrat al-Imam al-Khu'i." The project was successful and ambitious, a center to house, feed, and school orphans. Fadlallah's brother, Muhammad-Baqir, who holds a Ph.D. in chemistry from France, headed it. His orphanage was so prestigious and popular, that Hezbollah, under Iranian leadership, have started a similar institution called "Mu'assasat al-Shahid," (the Martyr's Institution.)

Contradictory Relations with the Iranian Republic

Fadlallah's relations with Iran were fraught with contradictions. Often at odds with Hezbollah, he still was a famous jurist who advocated political activism on the part of the Islamic people, a main ideological premise of the Iranian Revolution. Perhaps more paradoxical has been his posi-

[77] Fadlallah, "Nahtaj ila 'Uqul fiha": reference not traced

[78] Khaṭawāt 'alā Ṭarīq al-Islam (Beirut: Dār al-Ta'āruf, 1985); Qaḍāyānā 'alā Ḍaw' al-Islām (1973).

tion supporting the theory of "wilayat al-faqih" (sovereignty of the jurist), a concept central to Khomeini's thinking, while still being opposed to the notion that the ulama should run a government However, Fadlallah, the master politician, might be said to be playing it both ways.

While he advocated for al-Khu'i's marja'iya during the grand ayatollah's lifetime and influenced people to prefer al-Khu'i over Khomeini, he was given an ijaza to receive khums from Khomeini followers because of his influential position in Lebanon. This, in turn, strengthened his reputation among political activists, who, until that time, had accused him of being apolitical because of his support for al-Khu'i.

Fadlallah preserved his relationship with Iran through rocky times by publicly supporting the Islamic Republic of Iran and its leading role in the Islamic world. Whether the Iranian government liked his views or not, they found it necessary (or beneficial) to invite him to public and political events and to the religious conferences that are held frequently in Iran. His prestige increased considerably in Iran when the Western media portrayed him as the spiritual leader of those who bombed the American and French barracks in late 1983.

Yet Fadlallah has not shied away from criticism of the regime in Iran. Tensions mounted between Fadlallah and Iran after the death of Khomeini when Iran tried to "appoint" the elderly, and by some accounts senile, 'alim, Araki. The death of al-Khu'i set off another round of tensions when Fadlallah advocated for the marja'iya of Gulpaygani, in spite of the fact that he had not always seen eye to eye with the great ayatollah in Qom. Fadlallah had written that the offices of marja'iya and wilaya should be separate, implying that the jurist-leader of Iran may not have any influence in the choice of the marja'. In retaliation for his refusal to back Khamene'i as the marja', at least one faction of the Iranian government publicly discredited Fadlallah as a jurist.

Fadlallah's Quest for the Marja'iya

After the death of al-Khu'i, Fadlallah's opinion was sought as to who should be supported as the grand ayatollah's successor. As we have seen, Sistani was generally proclaimed in Najaf to hold that distinction. Fadlallah expressed his support for Sistani, but, true to form, he qualified his support with the statement that Sistani was one of many high-ranking jurists in Najaf and Qom. Indeed, he added, he did not see Sistani as being more knowledgeable than himself. As we saw in Chapter four, Khamene'i's candidacy for the marja'iya was very much a non-starter as the senior jurists in the hawza in Qom did not take him seriously.

Therefore, the confusion that reigned after the death of al-Khu'i, compounded by the Gulf War which left Najaf in a virtual state of siege by the Iraqi government, appeared to provide a window of opportunity for Fadlallah to rise to prominence as a marja', at least among his followers. But Fadlallah was cautious about taking a public stand. A group of his followers approached him with a list of more than two hundred questions. By taking on the challenge of answering them he would be proclaiming his marja'iya. Initially, he refrained from agreeing to this request, replying that the time was not yet ripe to announce his candidacy. It was apparent that he was surveying the extent of his popularity and the reaction that the religious establishment would have to his ambitions.

However, in 1994, he published his *al-Masa'il al-Fiqhiya* (Questions on Islamic law), a book that by its existence makes Fadlallah a contender for the marja'iya. A year after its publication it was in its fourth edition. The success of this book, which might be called a pseudo-legal manual, is due to its simple style in presenting religious laws. Fadlallah departed from the traditional style of obtuse writing. It is in a question and answer format and is a collection of questions sent to Fadlallah requesting his juristic opinions.

Aside from its straightforward style, it also has the advantage of addressing issues of real concern to the believers in their lives. In fact, people who would not be muqallid to Fadlallah acquired his book and some of those who may have started out being muqallid to someone else turned to Fadlallah because of the appeal of this text.

The other advantage of this book is that Fadlallah, if he deemed it necessary, could have denied that it was truly a risala. In other words, he could still have claimed that he was not seeking the marja'iya. As we have seen, it is unwise for an 'alim to put forward his marja'iya too soon, and he opens himself up to criticism by doing so. And, in fact, he did not escape criticism from his colleagues. Despite the popularity of his book, traditional ulama are critical of him for not producing the standard legal manual or juristic work to prove his standing in fiqh and usul. In response, Fadlallah began to publish his work on fiqh, based on lectures he had delivered to his students in his hawza in Beirut and in Damascus. Yet, still he refrained from actually publishing a full-fledged risala. Instead, he says, he has let it be known that his legal rulings will be in the format of footnotes to al-Sadr's risala, *al-Fatawa al-Wadiha*, a text that also does not follow the classical style. By footnoting al-Sadr's risala, of course, Fadlallah is making the statement that he sees himself al-Sadr's successor.

Fadlallah's Reforms

Like Baqir al-Sadr before him, Fadlallah wished to reform and redefine the marja'iya. Like al-Sadr, Fadlallah wanted an institution in the truest sense—or stated differently, he wanted a marja'iya, not a marja'.

Fadlallah emphasized that he envisioned a marja'iya that was not limited by political boundaries, but rather reflected the interests and concerns of the entire Islamic umma. Having witnessed the active role of Pope John Paul II with his worldwide travel and his broad appeal to the masses, Fadlallah was advocating that the marja' should not only have the spiritual and intellectual capacity to carry out his duties, but also the physical stamina to lead and to be with his followers.[79] The marja' should not, according to Fadlallah, be confined to his religious quarters in Najaf or Qom, but should pay visits to communities and try to influence the policies of political regimes to make them conform to Islamic teachings.

Of course, such ideas run counter to the structure of the Iranian government. At this point, the Iranian government would like to see the wilayat al-faqih and the marja'iya as one, so long as the person who holds the position is in agreement with the ideology of the regime. It must be mentioned that the marja', if he resides in Iran, is circumscribed in his activities by virtue of being a member of a state that is considered anathema to most of the world's governments. Moreover, regardless of external political pressures on Iran, the ideology of the Islamic Republic is very nationalistic and it seems reasonable to assume that any marja' in Iran would be principally concerned with the Iranian government and society.

Fadlallah's Future[80]

What were the chances of Fadlallah being recognized as a marja'? There were a number of factors working against him. First and foremost, he was too involved in politics to have a very broad appeal. As we have seen, one of Sistani's main strengths was the fact that he does not involve himself in political activity.

Another hindrance to his rise in station was the mere fact that he resided in Lebanon. While Fadlallah was a graduate of Najaf, he lived in the Middle Eastern city most renowned for its decadence and secularism: Beirut. Not only was it a city with a large Christian population, but also it had also just pulled itself out of a sixteen-year-long bloody civil war. Its very name conjured up images of corruption of all sorts. A marja' residing in such a place would be discomfiting indeed. Never has Beirut been

[79] Muḥammad-Ḥusayn Faḍl Allāh and Salīm al-Hasanī, *al-Ma'ālim al-Jadīda li'l-Marja'īya al-Shī'īya* (Beirut: Dār al-Malāk, 1993), and Muḥammad-Ḥusayn Faḍl Allāh, *al-Marja'iya al-Waqi'*: reference not traced.

[80] JW: This section was written was written in the mid-1990s—prior to Fadlallah's death in 2010. I have left it as it was written in the mid-1990s, and I have not tried to update it, apart from putting the verbs into the past tense.

associated with the sacred or with Islamic learning. But would a change of residence have really helped Fadlallah? That is highly unlikely. An Iranian cleric said that the Iranian government tried to persuade him to move to Iran, but he rejected the idea. Had Fadlallah gone to Iran, he would probably have suffered the fate of other activist ulama who did not see eye to eye with the government, such as Muntaziri, Ruhani, and Shirazi. Najaf would also be out of the question for obvious reasons.

Fadlallah has no prominent students. As we have seen, the number and the prominence of one's students is an important factor in spreading one's reputation as a marja'. While one may gain renown in other ways, having one's students carry one's name far and wide is considered a legitimate way to promote a marja'iya.

Many of his views are far from the mainstream. His assertion that there is no historical basis for certain closely-held Shi'i beliefs, such as 'Umar's harsh treatment of Fatima, antagonizes most ulama. They have, as we have seen, even felt compelled to speak out against him publicly.

There is an even more central reasons, however, why Fadlallah could never be widely accepted among the Shi'a as a marja'. In people's minds he is associated with militancy, violence, and divisiveness. Khomeini's heritage notwithstanding, the vast majority of Shi'a do not want a politicized religion.

However, as we have seen, the ambivalence of the position of the marja' sometimes works in the favor of someone such as Fadlallah. He can continue to garner support for himself and for his ideas through his writings and activities. He may never be recognized as the grand marja' of the Shi'i world, yet, he might very well become powerful enough to force changes in the institution. His source of power may actually come from an active, educated, and articulate group of Shi'a who are seeking reforms, which include more say in the way their religion is run and less obeisance to the ulama. We will look again at Fadlallah's influence when we discuss the marja'iya in the West in chapter eight.

Chapter Seven

Sistani: The Imprisoned Marja'

SOME OF THE ULAMA were imprisoned during the uprising following the Gulf War. They were brought a pot of soup. Because this soup was presented by corrupt people, they discussed whether or not to eat it. Finally, one 'alim said that he would accept it and then presented it to the rest so that it would be pure for them. They ate and then the door to their cell was opened and in poured a horde of prisoners. The prisoners were permitted to take one scoop of the soup. If they tried to take more, they would be beaten with a baton. This was a horrifying experience for the ulama, who felt very guilty for having eaten it.[81]

IF YOU VISIT THE HOMES of Iraqi ulama or members of ulama families, your eyes are likely to gravitate to a framed photograph of an 'alim. Or, the frame may contain several small photographs. No inquiry is usually necessary to learn who these men are, as this information will be volunteered freely. They are—or had been—prisoners in Iraq's jails. Usually, their fate is unknown. However, judging from reports of people who somehow have been freed, their prospects for being alive are practically nil. After the 1991 Gulf War, Saddam's forces rounded up hundreds of Iraqi ulama and threw them in jail.

Ayatollah Sayyid 'Ali Sistani was among the ulama arrested. He was born in Mashhad, Iran, in 1930 to a clerical family. He studied in Qom under Borujirdi and at the age of twenty-two went to Najaf where he

[81] Told to me by an anonymous source who personally knew the ulama in prison.

studied under al-Hakim , Husayn al-Hilli, and al-Khu'i. There are two important facts about him. First, he continued to be identified as an Iranian, even into the 1990s. Second, he was known to be completely apolitical. When asked why Sistani would have remained silent even during the horrendous days of the Intifada of 1991 after the Gulf War in, some informants say it was because he was Iranian and did not think it was suitable for him to be involved in an Iraqi matter. Other informants state that Sistani is so scholarly and detached from the world that he does not even read a newspaper, in which case, the matter of which government he lived under would be immaterial to his political quietism.

One of my informants said that, when Sistani was in jail, he was recognized by a guard, who was described as being "courageous." The guard said that Sistani "is just like al-Khu'i," and with this commendation, Sistani was released. What to make of this situation is difficult to decide. Was it the guard's admiration for al-Khu'i that benefitted Sistani? Or, was it the fact that he was Iranian—a high-ranking mujtahid who would not be a threat to the Iraqi government? Is it possible that they thought he could be manipulated to be on their side? He was a student of al-Khu'i's, after all, and the government could have presumed that he would not have affection for the Islamic Republic of Iran. As mentioned in chapter five, the governments of Iraq and Iran were persistently attempting to co-opt the marja'iya and bring it under government control. Perhaps they had hopes that Sistani would be amenable to their persuasion.

Sistani was released from jail, while many other ulama were incarcerated and never released. A profile written about Ayatollah Sistani says, "He excelled his peers, especially in the forcefulness of his interjections, his quick wit, his prolific research in jurisprudence, biographies of transmitters, and his keeping abreast with many theories in different fields of theological sciences." Yet, informants who knew him in Najaf, though they never speak a disparaging word about him, say that he was one of many very learned ulama of his generation and that no one expected that he would be especially singled out to be the grand marja' in Najaf one day.[82]

Today, though, he is the marja' to whom the majority of Shi'a are muqallid. In spite of Iran's prestige as a Shi'i government, Iran's maraji' cannot compare in influence with Sistani. Though I came to this conclusion through numerous interviews with people who reside in North America, Great Britain, and the Middle East, the novel indicator of Sistani's popularity was provided by an 'alim who had just returned from

---

[82] *Al-Noor,* 1993: reference not traced.

Mecca. He stated that, "Before someone makes hajj, he should pay khums to the wakil of the marja'. The person actually pays this in Mecca. Each marja' has an office in Mecca. If he does not pay khums, he is told that his pilgrimage is not acceptable to God. You look at the office of each marja' to see whose line is longest. The line at Sistani's office is the longest." (Other argue that since Sistani residing in Iraq which was under international embargo, there was no means to transfer khums to his office, so the only way to do so is in Mecca during the hajj.)

Sistani's rise was not something to be taken for granted. We have seen how instrumental students are in promoting a marja', yet Sistani was under observation by the Iraqi government and had virtually no students, so that the usual avenues for building one's reputation as a great mujtahid were closed to him. Additionally, Sistani did not produce major religious writings, either in jurisprudence (fiqh and usul) or in theology, Quranic studies, or philosophy. His only intellectual work is limited to written lectures on *al-'Uurwa Wuthqa* of Kazim Yazdi; others are merely booklets on jurisprudence or his legal opinions as part of the manual of law. Understanding how and why Ayatollah Sistani rapidly became the grand marja'—in a world where there were several aspirants to the position—helps us to understand the marja'iya, the significance it has in the lives of the Shi'a, and the impact that world events have and continue to have on the institution.

Making Sistani a Marja'

Sistani is often referred to by the people who are muqallid to him as al-Khu'i's successor in Najaf. In fact, the gloss frequently put on his marja'iya today is that he was handpicked by the illustrious late grand marja' himself. This is in keeping with the idea that once someone is recognized as a marja'—especially as a grand marja' with a very broad based following—his marja'iya is made to seem inevitable and self-evident. One 'alim who was interviewed said that Ayatollah al-Khu'i seems to have wanted Sistani as the marja' because "he gave signs such as asking him to lead prayers and to give lectures in his absence."

In the same "Profile" of Sistani cited above, the author stated that "After the passing away of al-Sayyid al-Khu'i, he was among the six persons who took part in his funeral, and performed the service on the dead body." This can be read in two ways. Obviously, the author wanted to illustrate the high respect shown to Sistani. Performing the service at a funeral is, as we have seen, an indicator that one is being looked upon as a successor. On the other hand, he was one of six to have had such an honor, an indicator that he was not without peers—either inside or outside of prison.

As we have seen, Sistani's accession to the marja'iya was not so automatic as we might be led to believe. The fact that in 1994 the Imam Al-Khoei Islamic Foundation requested the late Ayatollah Gulpaygani to "supervise" its activities indicates that even al-Khu'i's own relatives did not immediately turn to Sistani. And, as pointed out earlier, the Al-Khoei Foundation did not immediately follow Gulpaygani either.

There is no one specific answer to the question of how Sistani became the most widely followed marja' in the Shi'i world. The answer to this question will have to be addressed from a variety of perspectives. In this chapter we will focus on how communities and individuals in Western countries have influenced the selection of a marja' who was "accidently," as one informant put it, released from an Iraqi prison and was then virtually studentless while under close official surveillance.

The Iraqi government continued its policy of trying to interfere with the selection of the marja'. Saddam was obviously successful, as was the Shah of Iran in his time, in co-opting a few of the clergy. The Iraqi government was quick to favor its own candidate to the position, Sayyid Muhammad al-Sadr, a cousin of Baqir al-Sadr who, reportedly, was called in to identify latter's body after his execution. Oddly enough, he is from a family with two renowned religious leaders who had much to say about the role of religion and politics. Anyone wishing to study in Najaf—and, consequently, avoid the draft—had to seek permission from al-Sadr. Interestingly, when an 'alim living in the United States was questioned about Muhammad al-Sadr, he expressed surprise that al-Sadr would agree to cooperate with Saddam. He added that he had written "some good books" in the past and did not know what had happened to change him. This 'alim said confidently that the people would not follow al-Sadr, but would follow Sistani instead.

Al-Sadr's chances of being considered the marja' quickly dissipated when Muhammad al-Sadr acted independently of the dictates of the government and issued a fatwa requiring Shi'ites to attend Friday prayers. Friday prayers are not considered a required ritual in Shi'a jurisprudence. It was a bold step to show his activism and distance himself from the government of Saddam. Since all public Shi'a religious rituals were banned by Saddam, especially after the 1991 Intifada, attending Friday prayers became a symbolic activism for the shi'a to show their commitment to their faith as well as their resistance to Saddam regime. Such populism made him a hero, and al-Sadr rose high in the esteem of the Shia masses. He then began to challenge other maraji' in Najaf, especially Sistani and al-Hakim, calling them publicly the "silent marja'iya" as opposed to his "vocal/activist marj'ya." Not since the 1906 Constitutional Revolution in Iran had there been such vocal criticism and public condemnation of one Shi'a cleric by another.

The result of this conflict was deep division among Iraqi Shi'a, with those following al-Sadr mostly from the masses of the poor and the followers of Sistani mostly middle-class. Such division with the Iraqis did not end with the violent death of al-Sadr in late 1999. It was widely believed that the death of al-Sadr and his two sons was the work of Saddam's security service, for al-Sadr had begun to use his sermons during Friday prayers to criticize oppressive government policies and actions against the Shi'a.[83]

With the death of Muhammad al-Sadr, the field was wide open for Sistani's marja'iya to spread among Iraqis. Moreover, political circumstances played major role in Sistani's favor. The isolation of Iraqis from the outside world due to the international sanctions imposed on Iraq as well as the great animosity of Saddam's regime toward Iran prevented Iraqi Shi'a from being influenced by or exposed to Fadlallah's marja'iya in Lebanon or Khamene'i's marja'iya in Iran. Other competing maraji' in Najaf, such as the Afghan Ishaq Fayyad, the Pakistani Bashir al-Najafi, and the Iraqi Sa'id al-Hakim lacked the international financial and media support provided by major institutions like the Al-Khoie Foundation and Khoja community in the West.

Sistani and the Al-Khoei Foundation

An Iraqi 'alim said, "The Al-Khoei Foundation needed a marja' and they found one in Sistani." What does this statement mean? What is the significance of being the marja' of a foundation established by a former marja'? How is the relationship sustained?

As mentioned earlier, it is in the by-laws of the Al-Khoei Foundation that the Board of Trustees is supposed to select a marja' to become affiliated with the Foundation. It is the marja' who says that an individual or organization can use religious money or property. The marja' sanctions the work of that individual or organization in the eyes of the people. So powerful is this idea among Shi'a—at least those who are accustomed to having their communities run by ulama—that even a Shi'i organization not funded by religious taxes, but simply by membership fees is subject to doubt and criticism if the money is used without the explicit approval of a marja'. For example, an organization founded by Shi'i students in the United States called The Muslim Group collects dues. The leadership felt

83 JW: The greatest legacy of Muhammad al-Sadr in Iraq in the post-Saddam era after 2003 is the rise of al-Sadr political movement, otherwise known as al-Ahrar, with its militant wing, the Jaysh al-Mahdi, which are led by his son, Muqtada.

it was entitled to spend that money on the needs of the organization as they saw fit. They emphasized accountability and record keeping to make sure that the books were in order and that there could be no question of dishonesty. Still, a large fraction of the members of the organization complained that the leaders had no right to spend this money as its expenditure had not been sanctioned by a marja'. The leaders of the organization complied with the pressure and turned to Fadlallah for his blessing.

Still, it is unusual for an organization to "elect" a marja' as the Al-Khoei Foundation has done. The marja'iya is a grassroots institution. While mujtahids give their opinions on who should be the marja', it is unusual for an institution not consisting of mujtahids to vote for a marja'. It is obvious, though, that before this vote took place, the grassroots part of the institution had been operating. The Board did not decide on Sistani overnight. Negotiations had to take place.

After the death of Ayatollah al-Khu'i, the Foundation found itself in an unusual and difficult position. The Foundation was established with the specific intention of financially sustaining the properties and endowments that had been started in the lifetime of Ayatollah al-Khu'i. Any community that established a school, mosque, hospital, or other institution in the name of al-Khu'i was openly expressing its loyalty to and respect for him. Other maraji' had built institutions in their names, but al-Khu'i's influence—and consequently the amount of khums he collected—was incomparably greater than anyone else's. It apparently seemed very logical at the time to have a foundation established bearing al-Khu'i's name, considering the amount of money involved in his marja'iya and the number of projects it initiated. But what about after his death? What does the foundation of a marja' do after the death of a marja'? Does the foundation transfer into the hands of the next grand marja', in which case should the foundation be renamed in honor of the successor?

Of course, one of the defining roles of the marja' is that he collects khums either directly or through his emissaries. Even when he is spending lavishly on support of students, institution building, and charities, it is quite likely that there will be a considerable amount of wealth left over that has not been spent or earmarked. Traditionally, this money, of which there is no official accounting, has remained with the family of the marja' after his death. However, the circumstances with the al-Khu'i money were different. Al-Khu'i was the grand marja' for millions of Shi'a throughout the world, including the oil-rich Gulf region. Therefore, particularly in the 1970s, he collected a far larger amount of money than any other marja' had ever done. For the family to inherit this much money seemed improper to many of the ulama as well as to others. Establishing a foundation was supposed to eliminate questions about the family growing rich on khums.

The Al-Khoei Foundation quickly developed a life and purpose of its own. Not only did it maintain the properties begun during the lifetime of al-Khu'i, but it also set goals for new projects and has an active political relations and human rights element. The Foundation is very much the result of the personalities of the people whose interests and concerns have shaped it. The Foundation soon found itself in something of a bind. On the one hand, it needed a marja' to give it religious legitimacy. It also found that due to mismanagement of funds by a relative who was discredited and no longer part of the Foundation, it could not continue to function without additional funds. These funds would have to come chiefly from religious taxes. The Al-Khoei Foundation, then, to operate effectively, would need to act as a representative to a marja' with the understanding that it would receive a portion of the money it collected. On the other hand, to turn it over to a marja' could easily change the dynamics and purpose of the institution. They needed to find a marja' who would allow them a fair degree of independence to carry out their work without interference.

Working out the details of such an arrangement takes time. The Foundation would have to be assured that the relationship would be satisfactory for them, yet they knew well that they could not afford to do what the Iranian government had attempted—to select someone simply because he was docile and agreeable. This would detract from their prestige. Besides, the al-Khu'is were raised in a household in which they understood the importance of following "the most learned mujtahid of the time." As long as Gulpaygani lived, they could not ignore him. (Sabzevari had also been alive when al-Khu'i died, but he and al-Khu'i were rivals, and so he was not really a logical contender.) So, finally, the Al-Khoei Foundation announced that Gulpaygani was their marja', but he died almost immediately thereafter, and the search had to begin again

There was definitely a logic to selecting Ayatollah Sistani. Sistani was a student of Ayatollah al-Khu'i and, though of Iranian background, was not connected with the Islamic Republic of Iran. He was well respected, extremely devoted to scholarship, and not at all involved in politics.

Of course, the Al-Khoei Foundation cannot just "select" someone. That person must desire the relationship as well. The question was, would it be beneficial to Sistani's marja'iya to be associated with the Al-Khoei Foundation? The immediate answer to this question is, yes. After all, the Al-Khoei Foundation has the distinction of carrying the name, and the prestige, of the most broadly followed marja' in the Shi'i world—

possibly in history. Because al-Khu'i's name is associated with so many projects, Sistani's association with these projects would only buttress his reputation. He would have clearly been perceived as "al-Khu'i's" successor.

Yet, things are not quite so simple as that. The benefits have to be balanced against certain disadvantages. To begin with, the name of the Foundation suggests that Sistani lives in the shadow of al-Khu'i. More importantly, however, the questions about the financial irregularities of the Al-Khoei Foundations had not been put to rest and had been a cause of concern to those involved in Sistani's marja'iya. Also, some of the members of the Al-Khoei Foundation were actively involved in political issues. Their opposition to Saddam Hussein was not hidden. They advocated for human rights reforms in Iraq and were in contact with all the opposition groups. Sistani, who distanced himself even from the uprising and who is Iranian anyway, expressed concern about this and insisted that those involved in politics not be directly involved in the day-to-day running of the Foundation.

Sistani has kept a relationship—though not always an easy one—with the Al-Khoei Foundation. He benefited from it. Yet, there could have come a time when he felt strong enough as a marja', independent enough of al-Khu'i's reputation, and disgruntled enough with the independence of the al-Khu'i people, that he would have wished to distance himself from them. But, certainly, the Al-Khoei Foundation was instrumental in his ascension.

There are other reasons for the relatively rapid growth of Sistani's prestige. A key was provided by someone associated with the Al-Khoei Foundation. He emphasized the importance of a particular Shi'i ethnic community—the Khojas. Among other things, he said that, if they had decided to follow Ruhani in Qom, the Iranian Government would probably not have placed him under house arrest. This rather astonishing statement is well worth some contemplation.

The Khojas

In the middle of the eighth century C.E. there was a disagreement among the Shi'a regarding the rightful successor to the Imamate. The descendants of those who followed the minority view of the succession broke away from those who would eventually be called Ithna-'Ashari (or Twelver) Shi'a and came to be referred to as Isma'ilis, so-called from the name of their candidate. The Isma'ilis were successful in setting up the powerful Fatimid Caliphate, which in turn helped spread Isma'ilism from North Africa to Sindh. When the Fatimid state began to disintegrate, the Isma'ilis suffered an internal conflict dividing them into two major branches, the Nizariya and the Musta'liya. The Indian Nizaris are generally referred to as Khojas. According to Abdul Aziz Sachedina,

> it is certain that the name Khoja is the phonetic corruption of the Persian title *khwaja* (master, teacher, respected, well-to-do person) given by the Persian Isma'ili missionary Pir Sadr al-Din to his Hindu Indian converts to Islam in the fourteenth century.[84]

Sachedina refers to the Khojas as a caste. Because they had to practice taqiya and hide their Islamic faith, they "retained their caste ideas inherited from their Hindu ancestors."[85] A commercial people, they have been conducting business between India and East Africa since the seventeenth century. In the nineteenth century Sayyid Sa'id, the Sultan of Oman, invited them to settle on Zanzibar, where he had established his capital, and on the mainland of East Africa.

The Khojas at issue here were followers of the Isma'ili Agha Khan, though by this time there were also Khojas who had become either Sunnis or Twelver Shi'a. Agha Khan III was known to

> have devoted much of his time and financial resources to consolidating and organizing the Nizari community, especially in South Asia and East Africa. He was particularly concerned with introducing socio-economic reforms that would transform his Shi'i Muslim followers into a modern, self-sufficient community with high standards of education and welfare. The successful attainment of these objectives, however, required an appropriate administrative organization.[86]

However, it seems that some of his flock chafed under his control and, in the last quarter of the 19th century, a group of Khojas who had been loyal to the Agha Khan involved the British courts in their complaints against him. These complaints centered on his rights to religious taxes. The British, who were on excellent terms with the Agha Khan, ruled in his favor. Those in disagreement with the court's decision seceded and joined the Khojas who had long since become Ithna-'Ashari. As Daftary comments, they were "the least organized group amongst the Asian immigrants to East Africa."[87]

The Ithna-'Ashari Khojas, many of whom have migrated to the United States, Canada, and England, may now be counted among the most organized religious groups in the world. The Khojas have an international organization called the World Federation of Khojas, with their

---

84 Reference not traced.

85 Reference not traced.

86 Farhad Daftary, *The Ismāʿīlīs: Their History and Doctrines* (2nd ed. Cambridge: Cambridge University Press, 2007), p. 484.

87 Reference not traced.

headquarters in London, England. In keeping with their ethos of a formal orderliness, they have a constitution that can only be amended through a voting procedure. The current president is El Hajj Mulla Asghar M. Jaffrey. Though he has a strong religious education, he was not trained at one of the hawzas in Iraq or Iran. The president is elected by the community every three years and is supposed to be limited to two terms. However, from records obtained from the Khojas, proposals were submitted and, obviously accepted, to continue his presidency.

The Khojas are deeply involved with philanthropic, educational, and religious activities, and they meticulously document both their activities and their financial dealings. For example, they have a Medical Advisory Board that is appointed by the President. The functions of the Board, as cited in a comprehensive portfolio on virtually all aspects of Khoja activities, are as follows:

> 1. To organise treatment of patients from all over the world.
>
> 2. To advise doctors and para-medics on post-graduate education in UK
>
> 3. To promote health education and provide relevant information to Jamaats and doctors of our community worldwide
>
> 4. To organize Haj Medical Mission.
>
> 5. To liaise with sister organizations in other countries, mainly third world and sending them medicines, equipment, journals, books and support and advice.
>
> 6. To organize medical screening programmes"

In addition, they have a Child Sponsorship Organization, an Islamic Education Board, an Advisory Board for Careers, Education and Training, and an International Rehabilitation Board, with their goals and objectives as clearly outlined as those stated above. A well-educated community of believers, they continue to be, as they were when first converted, prosperous and sophisticated. While there are divisions in the community—for example, a disagreement between the Khojas and at least one person on the Board of Directors of the Al-Khoei Foundation in London caused a rift in the Queens, New York community—they continue to have a caste identity and have a relatively high level of agreement and unity on important issues. While they do not exclude other Shi'a (or even other Muslims, for that matter), they see themselves as a religious/ethnic community separate from, though connected to, other Shi'a groups. The Khojas are open about wanting their own mosques and communities. As one Khoja informant said, "[The Khojas)] don't like Arabic food and Arabic ways of doing things. They want to start on time, for example, but the Arabs are always late." He added, "They don't like the Arabs' Muharram commemorations either," referring to the dramatic, colorful mourning ceremonies that are common among Middle Eastern Shi'a.

Ironically, while critical of the style and manner in which other Shi'a conduct their rituals and resistant to other cultural norms being imposed upon them, the Khojas are also the most ecumenical of Shi'a, actively promoting good relations with other religious groups. There is quite obviously a social class distinction at work here. Many of the Arab Shi'a who have come to North America are from poor backgrounds—often peasants from southern Lebanon and Iraq. Apart from their religious affiliation, the Khojas would have little in common with these people. On the other hand, the Khojas have no difficulty relating to other prosperous middle class religious groups. In Toronto, for example, a Khoja mosque shares a parking lot with a synagogue. The two congregations refer to it jokingly as "The Green Line," reflecting the cordial relations between the two. Also, when the Khojas interact with more highly educated Arabs or Iranians, such a sense of division is not apparent.

No other Shi'i ethnic group—be it Iranian, Lebanese, Iraqi, or Pakistani—defines itself quite so clearly as do the Khojas, nor do any other groups have such an organizational structure. Aside from the World Federation, there are regional and national organizations, such as the North American Shi'i Ithna-'Ashari Muslim Community. Other ethnic communities, while gravitating to one another because of linguistic or cultural factors ,do not integrate themselves in such a formal manner outside the workings of the larger Shi'i community. The Khojas also make hajj as a group and were, collectively, given the unusual permission by the Iraqi government to visit the holy shrines in Iraq.

The Khojas are a relatively small group, but their wealth, educational level, tightly controlled organization, and non-involvement in international politics all translate into disproportionate influence. One of their unique characteristics as a community is that they select a marja' as an independent community. As a leader in a Canadian Khoja community explained, "Mulla Asghari can recommend who the marja' should be, but a Khoja can decide against his candidate. However, most Khojas do follow him." Another Khoja, when asked how he chose his marja', replied,

> Ideally, you would search out the most learned *Khiber* of the time. When a marja' dies, he does not recommend a successor. So, all the mujtahids meet and decide. At the World Federation of Khojas the President [Mulla Asghar] is in touch with all the khibra and he reviews what they have come up with. He then personally chooses. He is the head of all the communities and the people will follow him. He becomes the representative and translates the marja''s writings.

As the leader of one North American mosque said, the Khojas tend to handle their problems locally, but when there is an issue that can't be settled locally, they will refer to the matter to Mulla Asghar as the leader of the group, as he is the only Khoja authorized to act on behalf of the marja'.

The Khojas, as a community, were muqallid to Ayatollah al-Khu'i. When, he died, they followed Gulpaygani, though he seems to have struck many of the Khojas as being too conservative in his views. The Khojas have a strong sense of the appropriateness of adapting to new surroundings. These are a people who are accustomed to settling new areas of the world and see the importance of being part of the larger society. For example, like Khomeini, Gulpaygani drew strict lines between the believers and non-believers (kafirs), so that contact between the two is very circumscribed. Such restrictions between Khojas and non-Muslims would be very difficult to put into practice. After all, the Khojas were merchants—and successful ones.

The Khojas' relations with Gulpaygani were apparently not very smooth for other reasons, as well. One of the deciding factors in following Gulpaygani was that he would allow the community independence, especially in regard to how to use the khums. However, according to my sources, problems arose when Gulpaygani's son, Muhammad-Jawad, would not allow the use of khums collected outside of Canada to be used for a school that the Khojas wanted to build in Canada. This was a source of contention for the Canadian Khoja community since they raised money for projects outside of North America and could not understand why they could not reverse this procedure. Among other things, this situation underscores the importance of sons in the marja'iya, as well as the way the use of khums is negotiated as part of the equation in the marja'/muqallid relationship.

With the death of Gulpaygani, the Khojas once again had to select a new marja'. As mentioned above, the Khojas had been muqallid to al-Khu'i, not to Khomeini. There are two reasons for this. First, and foremost, was the Khojas' insistence on remaining "outside of politics." By this is meant that they do not want to be seen as part of the politicization of Islam, which has been the direction that Iran has gone. Neither do they want to be involved with the activists among the Arab Shi'a. They might have sympathies with them, but they are adamant about keeping religion and current political affairs separate. As we have seen, al-Khu'i avoided political activities and, therefore, was always identified as the marja' for the apolitical Shi'a. Though Iranian, he also was strongly identified with Najaf. Hence, Najaf is the center to whom the Khojas continue to seek guidance in selecting a marja'. After the death of the grand marja', the mujtahids give their opinions as to whom the people should be muqallid. In the case of the Khojas, the president sends out a letter citing the opinions of the mujtahids. There is no vote among the mujtahids—rather the opinions of certain mujtahids are stated, and apparently ranked in order of their weight in this decision-making process.

Essentially, the Khojas select their marja' by selecting the mujtahids who are going to influence their decision most heavily. They did not turn to Qom and the Council of Experts. They did not turn to the ulama in Karbala. Rather, they referred to a group of mujtahids in Najaf for advice. Therefore, they are not only linked to the marja' that "Najaf" selected—in this case Sistani—but are principally linked to the network of Najafi ulama. This should not be interpreted as meaning that they are alienated from the rest of the ulama. However, it does suggest that they do not wish to be controlled by the Islamic Republic of Iran, nor do they wish to be identified with Iran's interpretation of Shi'ism and its leadership. However, they certainly do not denounce Iran. For example, to outsiders Khojas sometimes refer to Khamene'i as today's banner carrier for Shi'ism. It was perhaps revealing that in a community in northern England an Iranian 'alim, who claimed to have an ijaza from Khamene'i's, seemed to know nothing of the Khojas except that they were "standoffish" and didn't participate in the mosque with which he was affiliated. This attitude was in sharp contrast with that of the people at the Al-Khoei Foundation who spoke of the Khojas with great respect and had regular contact with them.

In fact, the Khojas' importance to the Shi'i community at large is far more significant than their numbers would indicate, whether other Shi'a want to recognize their significance or not. Their commitment to philanthropic activities that are carried out with missionary zeal, their highly literate, well-educated membership, and their independence from the political travails that other communities suffer give them the potential for having a great deal of clout. They are also among the most active Shi'a in initiating and carrying out educational classes for children and youth. For example, those Khojas who are affiliated with the Al-Khoei Foundation Mosque in Queens, New York (as opposed to the Khoja Mosque that is also in Queens) tend to be the religion teachers at that mosque. This puts them in an excellent position to strengthen the marja'iya. Yet, the sense is that they will not do so blindly. They demand control over their own community and activities. No marja' will succeed with them if he takes them for granted.

That Sistani has shown due respect is indicated in the ijaza he issued to Mulla Asghar. It reads,

> Be it known to all the Khoja Shia Ithna Asheri brothers that the respected scholar, competent preacher, and propagator of the laws of Shari'ah, Mulla Asghar Muhammad Jaffer. . . is permitted and allowed to spend, as much as he deems advisable, from the sehme Imam. . . and other religious dues which he collects, in accordance with the laid down laws and ways of Shari'ah, and to forward the remaining to me for the preservation and the establishment of hawzas.[88]

Sistani ends his ijaza with the words, "And I enjoin him [Mulla Asghar] not to forget me in his good prayers, especially at such places and times when the duas are heard, the same way I will not forget him, Allah willing." Once again we are reminded of the interdependence of the marja' and the muqallid.

[88] From the translation of the Ijaza issued by Ayatollah al-'Uzma Sayyid 'Ali Sistani to Mulla Asghar, President of the World Federation.

Chapter Eight

Building a Dynasty

EARLIER I DISCUSSED the role of the sons and sons-in-law of the maraji‘. Just as I had to address what happens to the khums the marja‘ leaves behind after his death, I also have to look at what happens to the family—especially the sons and sons-in-law—that he leaves behind.

Among Ayatollah al-Khu'i's sons, the most ambitious and active was Muhammad-Taqi. According to informants who knew him, he was the paramount diplomat and one of the major reasons why his father was so well known and so widely followed. It was he who was largely responsible for setting up the projects that either were built or were scheduled to be built in his father's name. Taqi al-Khu'i came to a premature and tragic end at the hands of Saddam's forces on July 22, 1994. However, the Al-Khoei Foundation had been established and various members of the al-Khu'i family continued to be involved in that endeavor. The Al-Khoei Foundation, first and foremost, allows the name and reputation of al-Khu'i to continue. His greatness lives on in spite of his death and not just as an historical figure. Like the Imams, he plays an active role in the lives of the Shi‘a as projects benefitting the community are established in his name. The descendents of al-Khu'i have a very active role in preserving this prestige.

Ayatollah Sistani, as the marja‘ of the Al-Khoei Foundation does not inherit the Foundation. His links to it are informal. He, as was stated above, gives legitimacy to the expenditures of the Foundation, yet this relationship does not eradicate the almost inevitable competition that arises between the family of the old marja‘ and the new marja‘ who is trying to build his own reputation. It is not necessarily Sistani who is involved in the competition—at least not directly—but rather his relatives and other representatives interested in promoting the Sistani name. How Sistani should handle this relationship with the Al-Khoei Foundation would not be easy to assess.

Sistani has already begun the process of distancing himself a bit from the Al-Khoei Foundation and has encouraged the payment of khums directly to him. He is, after all, the marja‘. Yet, the Al-Khoei Foundation can act as an intermediary, in which case it becomes a "secondary receiver" of khums. Whether khums would be paid through the Al-Khoei Foundation, directly to Sistani, or through some other representative is quite clearly something of a popularity contest. There are people who would have been muqallid to al-Khu'i for many years and would still feel an attachment to "their marja‘." Attachment to the memory of al-Khu'i might be sufficient reason for people to continue to want to pay their religious taxes to his foundation. Alternatively, people might simply wish to give to the Al-Khoei Foundation because they agree with its particular activities, just as they might give to any of the other organizations founded by the Shi‘a. These contributions would not be considered khums, yet they would still be used to sustain and enhance the Foundation.

Sistani—meaning his own relatives and representatives—must lure the followers away from the al-Khu'i people without being perceived as divisive. It is the role of the marja‘ role to unite the community, not to divide it. Furthermore, as noted above, Sistani has benefited immensely by being perceived as al-Khu'i's successor, so to alienate his family would not be to his benefit. The only reason why he would want to do so is if there were problems of mismanagement of funds or if the Foundation became a primarily political organization. One of the tasks of his representatives is to ensure that all is well on these fronts.

The situation with the al-Khu'i family is actually fairly simple and straightforward matter. There is a foundation and the family is relatively unified. The transition to acceptance of a new marja‘ seems to have been fairly smooth. However, there have been other maraji‘ in this century. What has happened to them?

The family of Ayatollah Muhsin al-Hakim is a particularly interesting and complex case. Ayatollah al-Hakim had more than one wife at a time, a rather unusual family arrangement among the Shi‘i clerics. As a consequence, he had many children. The sons who were the most consequential, though, are the ones he had by his Lebanese wife, the aunt of Shaykh Fadlallah of Lebanon. Earlier we mentioned that the sons of maraji‘ are often ulama themselves but do not achieve the status of their father in learning. Instead, they are more likely to be the intermediaries between their father and the people and to play a variety of administrative and diplomatic roles. Probably because al-Hakim had many sons, there was more of a chance that one of them would follow in his father's scholarly footsteps. Indeed, his son Sahib was considered a likely successor to al-Khu'i in the 1980s by both his family and others who knew him, though he was still quite young. Noted for his knowledge of fiqh and usul, he was both the son of al-Hakim and the student of al-Khu'i.

Sahib did not have the opportunity to fulfill his potential. In 1983 the government hanged six members of the al-Hakim family, among them the forty-one-year-old Sahib, as a warning to others not to carry out any revolutionary plans against Iraq.[89] During his lifetime Sahib al-Hakim was compared favorably to Baqir al-Sadr, who was also young when he began to draw followers and make his mark. The two men were similar in their interest in making the marja'iya into a strong force for social and political change. The possibility of the younger al-Hakim rising to the position of grand marja' gave hope for the future to the bereaved followers of Baqir al-Sadr, who had been executed five years earlier.

Though Muhsin al-Hakim did not have another son who was a realistic contender for the marja'iya, he did have other very noteworthy male offspring. One of them was Mahdi al-Hakim, the founder of al-Da'wa and the head of the Ahl al-Bayt Organization, now based in London. Mahdi al-Hakim was reputedly the real political leader in the family. He was as devoted to addressing Iraq's political problems as Khomeini was to Iran's. However, his attempts to change the Iraqi government did not please Iran. He was far too independent of the Islamic Republic of Iran, which wanted to control him and his organization. When he served as the representative of his father in Pakistan, he got to know people who would finance his own activities, especially in Dubai and in the United Arab Emirates. Mahdi al-Hakim was considered a possible political leader in Iraq, but he was killed in Khartoum, probably by Saddam's agents, in 1988. While the organizations he founded continue, Mahdi al-Hakim has never truly been replaced.

The Iranians had better luck with Muhammad-Baqir al-Hakim , the official "head" of SCIRI.[90] Khomeini was keen to co-opt the leadership of the Iraqi Shi'a and to bring them under his banner. Just as he was antagonistic towards any rivalry from other groups within Iran, including Islamic groups, Khomeini also did not wish to see an independent al-Da'wa succeed. For a while, he seems to have thought that Shirazi could deliver the Iraqi Shi'a for him. But Shirazi never had broad-based Iraqi support. In 1982 SCIRI was established as an antidote and has been very

---

89 Joyce N. Wiley, *The Islamic Movement of Iraqi Shi'as* (Boulder, Colo.: Lynne Rienner Publishers, 1992), pp. 60, 70.

90 Baram, "Radical Shi'ite Opposition."

much under the control of the Iranian government. Other than al-Hakim, all the rest of the leadership is Iranian and Persian speaking, and, consequently, not of great appeal to many Iraqis, in spite of its claims to representing "all the Muslim people of Iraq, Sunnis as well as Shi'a."[91] However, these claims did not stop Iraqi activists from starting another opposition group outside of Iranian control. A representative of SCIRI was active in forming the Iraqi National Congress with headquarters in London and American government support. When the Iraqi National Congress organized its first conference in Vienna in 1992, SCIRI members refused to attend.

Relations with Iran have apparently continued to be uneasy. According to the Arab newspaper *Al-Hayat,*[92] Muhammad-Baqir al-Hakim planned a "private visit" to Damascus to "discuss with Syrian officials the state of the Iraqi opposition and the possibility of moving permanently to Damascus." Syria reportedly wanted an alternative to the Western-backed Iraqi opposition coalition, the Iraqi National Congress (INC). It seems that relations between SCIRI and the Iranian government had soured by then as, in the same news story, there was a reference to the fact that Iran had announced it had closed down a camp for Iraqi Shi'ite refugees along the border because of Baghdad's complaint that it was being used to stage cross-border attacks inside Iraq.

Regardless of Iranian or other governmental interference, the Iraqi movements did not held together well. They appear to have been highly dependent on the charisma of the leader and did not develop strong infrastructures to guarantee their healthy survival after the death of the founders. Family divisions were endemic so that larger overriding goals tended to be lost in power struggles. While all ardently wished to have Saddam overthrown, they did not agreed on what should follow. Not only were there family divisions, but also there was tension between the ulama and the laymen who had different visions of what an Iraqi government should be. The differences here were not religious vs. secular, for most of the people involved were devoted Islamists. However, defining the term "Iraqi Islamist" was not a simple matter. They came in a variety of hues and shades, some of them being strict Usulis who advocatde the leadership of the ulama, while others seemed more like the Muslim Brothers of Egypt, with their anti-clerical stance.

Ultimately, though, kinship still appears to be the overriding factor in drawing lines of demarcation. A family that has had its leader reach the pinnacle of the clerical hierarchy is not going to easily give up its illustri-

---

91 Wiley, Islamic Movement, p. 60.

92 *Al-Ḥayāt,* 6 August 1995.

ous position. An ayatollah with the prestige of al-Hakim could, in terms of power and prestige, be likened to a king and his sons and daughters to princes and princesses. Both sons and daughters acknowledge that they are not treated as ordinary citizens, but rather in a very deferential manner. A daughter of a marja', for example, would be highly prized as a potential wife. Quite understandably, the family of the marja'would grow accustomed to this rank in society and would not expect to find themselves suddenly devoid of status. Also, the sons and sons-in-law would have most likely been engaged in activities related to the offices of the grand marja'. This would be their livelihood. Again, it would be highly unusual under such circumstances that the sons would simply close up shop and move on to another career path—especially since many of them would be at least middle-aged themselves. And just as family ties do not keep princes from fighting over power, they do not guarantee that the sons of the great ulama will not be in competition. Sons who take active roles politically stand a particularly good chance of finding themselves with their own set of followers and a different agenda from that of their brothers. For example, those who were aligned with the late Mahdi al-Hakim, the founder of al-Da'wa and the head of Ahl al-Bayt, would find themselves at odds with Muhammad Baqir al-Hakim of the Iranian-dominated SCIRI. Ernest Gellner states that in the Middle East "there is a permanent tension between the two principles of legitimacy, the egalitarian-scripturalist and the kin-based mediationist."[93] Even among the theologian-scholars we see the tension between placing law above all else and the "seduction of kinship."

The al-Hakims and al-Khu'is face the dilemma of being survivors of two maraji'. Al-Hakim and al-Khu'i each had his own separate institutions and offices and his own money to distribute. Each inspired intense devotion. None of these things evaporates after the death of the marja'. The families of the maraji' continue to want to sustain the legacy of their respective leader. This desire leads to a situation where the families vie with one another for prestige. The very nature of the institution as it exists today makes this situation all but inevitable. Since there is no Office of the Grand Marja', there is no bureaucracy in place to allow for a transition from one marja' to another. In other words, people are muqallid to a marja', not to the marja'iya itself. It is not like the papacy where there is an office and a vote that places the new man into that office. It might be said that there is no marja'iya—only a marja'—and there may be more than one of them at anytime. In a sense, it could be argued that a particular marja' does not actually die until all the family involved in his

[93] Gellner, "Tribalism."

business are dead. The family of the grand marja‘ preserves his reign for as long as possible after his death. Actually, since families are keenly aware of their genealogies, this competition can continue for many decades, even centuries. While Saddam Hussein has taken the lives of many of al-Hakim's and al-Khu'i's families, there are still survivors who sustain the reputations of their respective leaders.

For the al-Hakims and the al-Khu'is, the rivalries inherent in their peculiar situation has been exacerbated by the politics of the region. Muhammad-Baqir al-Hakim, the most prominent survivor in the family, stood squarely in Khomeini's court and supported those who were critical of al-Khu'i, openly criticizing his anti-political views and the fact that he still had channels of communication with the Pahlavis. (For example, al-Khu'i agreed to meet with the empress when the Shah was attempting to have his religiosity certified in an attempt to hold onto his throne.)

While Khomeini jealously guarded his prestige and power during his lifetime, the situation for his family has been of a somewhat different. There is no issue of leftover khums here. Since Khomeini served as the representative of the Imam and as the head of the state, the Imam's money passed directly to the state rather than into the hands of the family or a foundation in Khomeini's name. As we have seen, establishing the marja‘ as the leader of government has definite pitfalls, but it at least settles the issue of where the khums goes after the death of the marja‘. Whether the system of linking religious and temporal leadership could totally eliminate family competition is in question. While there should no longer be large sums of money at issue, there is still family pride to be considered. Governments in the Middle East are famous for being run by extended families. Yet, the fact that the khums goes to the government and not to the family would seem to be a countermeasure against the intense sort of inter-family rivalry that can exist with the traditional marja‘iya.

Encouraging the Muqallids in the West

Thus far we have spoken about how select national and ethnic groups and an important foundation have helped promote the marja‘iya of Ayatollah Sistani. They are certainly not alone in affecting the outcome of the competition for the marja‘iya. Other groups, in particular the Lebanese, are also important players in the establishment of the marja‘iya, both in their homeland and in the West. At this point, we wish to illustrate the dynamics of spreading the marja‘iya in the West. Since the marja‘iya is a grassroots organization, what goes on in Najaf and Qom is actually no more important than what occurs in Detroit, Toronto, Los Angeles, or London. Yet the importance of the West in the development of the marja'iya is a very recent development and not well recognized.

I did field work among the Lebanese Shi'a of Dearborn, Michigan. As I report in my book on that community, these Shi'a were in a transitional stage due to the influx of Lebanese escaping the ravages of civil war.[94] Linked with the war was the revivalism of Shi'ism in that country. The immigrants who had come before the war were far less expressive of their particular Muslim identity. Even though they had built a Shi'i mosque in the early 1960s, they did not emphasize those practices and beliefs that can make Shi'ism seem so alien to Sunni Islam. One of those beliefs was the marja'iya. Post-1975 immigrants, having been exposed to the Islamization process, tended to have at least heard of the marja'iya, if they weren't already devout followers of a marja'. The first step was in explaining the importance of the marja' to the potential muqallid.

The Mosque and the Marja'

Before proceeding with a discussion of the spread of the marja''s reputation in Western communities, it may be helpful to clarify some of the terms used. In North America, as in Lebanon and Iraq, it is more common to find Shi'i centers than it is to find mosques. There are definite advantages to having an Islamic center (which can be considered a Husayniya, a place where the death of Imam Husayn is commemorated) rather than a mosque, the most important being that a mosque is officially a religious endowment and, as such, can never be sold for any other purpose. If the mosque does not flourish or if it turns out to be inadequate for any reason, then the community is stuck with it. A center, on the other hand, may simply be a business building converted into a place for the community to gather. As such, it can be sold if necessary.

There is another benefit, although how much of a concern this is to people is questionable: women can enter Islamic centers at anytime without fear of ritually polluting the place during menstruation, while this is a concern in a mosque. However, women still did not participate in the activities at the Husayniyas in the Middle East, even though pollution was not an issue. Women frequently attend activities at the centers in North America for a variety of reasons. My previous research in the Lebanese community in Michigan found that women's position appeared to be enhanced by their involvement in the mosques, especially when they could plan and carry out events. However, this might not be the case for other nationalities of Shi'i women. Iraqi women, though not in the mosques and Husayniyas, could serve as wa'iz and give sermons in the

[94] Linda Walbridge, Without Forgetting.

homes. This is particularly interesting because through their sermons they are recognized as having a great deal of influence over the selection of the marja'. This is obviously a subject that deserves more research.

The lay Shi'a themselves tend to use the terms mosque and center interchangeably. Therefore, we will use the term mosque, though we are often, though not necessarily always, referring to centers. The al-Khu'i mosques in London and Queens, New York, are bona fide mosques, though the one in London was a synagogue that has been refurbished so that today it is easily identifiable as a mosque.

Not surprisingly mosques in the West are not run by mujtahids. Neither do mujtahids give the sermons or read prayers. The men who perform these jobs are the lower-ranking clergy. Musawi explains that

> below the lowest rank of mujtahids, there are diverse groups of the religious class who are generally called mulla or ruhani. They are divided according to the function that they perform: pishnamaz (leader of the daily prayers), wa'iz (preacher), mudarris (regular instructor) and rawdakhwan (reciter of religious tragedies.)"[95]

In the United States the terminology is a bit different. In the American Shi'i community, especially among the Lebanese, the terms shaykh and imam are often used interchangeably. The use of the term "imam" in such a context is highly controversial among Shi'a. The word "imam" simply means "in front of." Sunnis use this term for their ulama: the imam is the person who is in the front of the group leading prayers. For Shi'a the word has a sacred connotation because of the twelve Imams of Shi'ism, who were sinless and infallible. Some, especially religious Iraqis, feel that to use the term to describe a caretaker of a mosque or a preacher insults this concept. Ulama who attain high leadership positions such as Khomeini and Baqir al-Sadr are frequently spoken of by this title, yet the faithful on occasion express some misgivings about its use even with such outstanding individuals.

Another term that is used is "sayyid," indicating that the 'alim, who can be identified by his black turban, is a descendent of the prophet. This is a term that carries a high status and thus is preferred over any other title with the exception of Ayatollah. (An ayatollah who is also a Sayyid will be referred to as "Sayyid Ayatollah.")

The terms wa'iz, khatib, and rawdakhwan are often used interchangeably. These are the itinerant preachers who are highly skilled in oratory. Their services are in great demand, especially during the mourning months of Muharram and Safar, during Ramadan, and on Arba'in, the fortieth day after the death of Husayn. As Khuri found in Bahrain,

---

95 Kazemi Musawi, "Institutionalization," p. 297.

Iraqi ulama are particularly in demand for these occasions, and especially those from Karbala.[96]

Promoting the Marja' in the Mosque

Ulama lower than the rank of mujtahid are not supposed to advise people directly about whom they should follow, as they lack the formal qualifications to do so. Of course, most Shi'a living in the West do not have easy access to any level of mujtahid. They are fortunate to have any trained ulama living in their towns. Therefore, the ulama of a local mosque have more status and responsibility in a community in North America or Great Britain than they would have had in the Middle East because of the relative fewness of their numbers and their remoteness from the centers of Shi'ism. They are likely to be called upon in many capacities that they would not have had had they not migrated. This includes being consulted about the choice of marja'.

The Shi'i ulama in America have been born, raised, and educated outside the West. Those from Iran and the Arab world have been trained in the theological seminaries, primarily Najaf, but also in Qom, Isfahan, Karbala, and Mashhad. They have travelled to the West for a variety of reasons: persecution at home, a desire to spread Islam, the promise of opportunity to establish a place and a reputation for oneself without having to go through the twenty years or so of training that is usual to become a mujtahid. So, they attempt to find a niche in North American, Great Britain, and other places outside of the traditional Shi'i world.

Religious leaders among other ethnic groups—Khojas, Indians, and Pakistanis—typically study at the hawza for two to three years. They tend to focus attention on becoming good orators. Among the Khojas there are ulama who also have advanced degrees from Western universities, some of them with Ph.D.s in Islamic studies, so that they seem to be able to fluctuate between an insider's and an outsider's perspective with relative ease. Their experience as mosque leaders appears to be very much like that of a Presbyterian minister's in modern day America. His life does not seem to be so clearly defined by his religious role. An Iraqi Shi'i 'alim, for example, is almost never seen without his robes and turban and rarely does he have activities outside of those involving his religious affairs in one way or another. This is not usually the case among the Khoja ulama, who are not easily identified as ulama and who frequently have other occupations aside from their religious duties. However, there is a shortage of Khoja ulama in the West, so that the Khojas tend to rely on

---

[96] Khūrī, *Tribe and State*, pp. 72–81.

ulama from India or Pakistan because the medium for the majlis mourning rituals is Urdu for all of them.

How does one actually go about establishing himself in this new situation? One way is to be invited by the mosque, often by the mosque's board of directors, to fill a gap in leadership. The board of directors of the first Shi'i mosque in Detroit, the Islamic Center of America, has invited numerous ulama from abroad to take over the place of the mosque's founder, Shaykh Chirri. In the 1980s Shaykh Chirri was very elderly and had become senile, so it was apparent to all that he needed a successor. One after another, ulama from Lebanon or Iran arrived to fill his place. Each quarreled with the board and left to start his own mosque. The Islamic Center of America never relied on the marja' for financial assistance, principally because the board was highly assimilated into American life and wished to be independent.[97] However, the ulama had no such Americanizing experience. They had come from the places where the marja' was revered. To them he was the fountainhead of learning and the symbol of piety and goodness. And, even if the marja' was not revered by a particular 'alim for these qualities, he was undeniably a potential source of money to open a new mosque.

A shaykh cannot simply go to the marja' with an outstretched hand for khums. There are great demands on the resources at the disposal of the the marja', and even al-Khu'i's funds were not unlimited. The shaykh must prove that he is a good risk, that he will be able to attract enough followers who will be muqallid to that marja'. He must also show that he will teach proper Shi'i behavior. A marja' would not wish to be identified with a mosque that does not demand hijab, at least head coverings, some level of segregation of the sexes in the mosque, and generally a responsible attitude towards following all religious law. He does not wish to be linked to a mosque or a shaykh who bends to the demands for laxity in such matters.

Furthermore, because the shaykhs themselves have been trained in a religiously strict manner, they too wish to see the Shari'a enforced in their mosques. They respect and are part of the tradition of the ulama and the theological universities. At least initially, the ways of the West are as alien to them as they are to the marja' back in Najaf or Qom. Therefore, it behooves them to find a core of followers who are concerned with following religious law, including following a marja'in other words, people whom they don't have to convert to these ideas. A shaykh who can demonstrate his effectiveness in gathering around him a group of followers dedicated to living according to Islamic law will have a much better

[97] Linda Walbridge, *Without Forgetting*, pp. 63–64.

chance of receiving a sympathetic ear than someone who does not draw such a group. Of course, these are the same people who are liable to take responsibility for paying their religious taxes. With evidence that he has such a following, he may then convincingly go to the marja' and request funds to open a mosque or an Islamic center.

His challenges hardly end there. The shaykh new in the West must, if he is to survive, appeal to a larger group than those who accept a strict and narrow definition of Islamic law. The dilemmas that Muslims find themselves facing in the West are sometimes daunting, and the unsympathetic shaykh will not inspire affection and loyalty among a people already feeling overwhelmed by personal, financial, or social problems.

What does a man do, for example, if he is required to shave his beard in order to be employed? Is he permitted to shave it in spite of his desire to follow religious law? What about the woman who finds employment in a profession where hijab would be frowned upon if not considered an out-and-out hindrance to performing her job? Can she bend the rules about head coverings and still be considered a good Muslim?

The shaykh finds himself struggling to assist, and to appeal to, people who find it hard to abide by every law even if they still desire to remain within the bounds set by religious law as defined by the mujtahids. For many of these people, the teachings of the marja' seem antiquated and unhelpful in making the transition to a new life outside of the Dar al-Islam. If the shaykh were to attempt to strictly enforce the marja''s rulings, he will only add more hardships in the lives of people who are struggling to be "good Muslims" while also attempting to live amicably and successfully in Western society. The shaykh or the wakil who is understanding and flexible is highly valued. The words of a well-educated and devout Muslim from Canada are helpful in understanding the thinking of many like-minded people:

> Wakils help 'rationalize' a situation in which believers do things against fatwas. Also, the believers bank on the mercy of God. Rationalizing is rampant, especially outside of the Muslim world. Most maraji' don't understand the dilemmas facing the Muslims in the West. People like Shaykh S. and Sayyid M. are very helpful because they try to explain to the maraji' the types of difficulties that the believers face. Shaykh S. has stated that if a situation is unbearable for the believer, then it is allowable to do what he feels he needs to do. However, the use of loopholes is problematic because others are aware that you are doing this and are often critical of you for 'compromising' your principles.

Even more challenging are the Shi'a who are not at all oriented towards a legalistic approach to Islam and are simply guided by traditional values, which, in fact, may be contrary to the rulings of the marja'. The shaykh is likely to encounter all categories of believers in his work. Those who appear to be most successful are the ones who consider all elements of the community to be important, avoid using a critical manner with people, and develop a high level of diplomatic skills.

It is a point of pride among the leaders of three of the Shi'i mosques in California, (all led by members of the Qazwini family, who fled from Iraq to Kuwait and then, during the Revolution, left for Iran) that their congregations are so diverse, including Arabs of different nationalities, Iranians, Afghans, and Pakistanis, among others. Not only are they diverse in terms of their nationality, but also in terms of their practice of religion. In the United States an imam must cast a wide net to establish a viable mosque. Narrow views on religious legalities are rarely well received by the majority of the Shi'i population.

The Issue of Multiple Maraji'

The imam of the American mosque faces a dilemma about how to promote the marja'iya and how to advance the marja'iya of one individual. He may himself be muqallid to a marja' or even be a wakil or representative of a particular marja', but again it does not behoove the imam of an American mosque to promote one marja' too ostensibly. It is especially important not to do so in these days.

During the time that Shi'ism has grown so greatly in the West, the competition has become far more consequential: al-Khu'i vs. Khomeini; Sistani vs. Khamene'i, etc. Using the mosque as a direct means of promoting a particular marja', therefore, is a delicate business. The shaykh does not want to overstep his religiously prescribed bounds, nor does he want to alienate his congregation or potential congregants. Therefore, he might suggest a list, perhaps only two or three mujtahids, telling the people that these are the mujtahids most highly respected among their peers and most broadly followed.

Even in Islamic centers that are the official offices of a marja', this practice is carried out. For example, the Islamic Educational Center of Orange County in Irvine, California, is also the American head office of Grand Ayatollah Sayyid al-Ruhani, yet the imam of the mosque, Sayyid Mustafa Qazwini, appears quite comfortable with the fact that his congregants follow Ayatollahs Sistani, Shirazi, and Qomi, aside from Ruhani. Interestingly, there are among this group followers of Mirza Ihqaqi, the Shaykhi marja' of Kuwait, who has financed some important Shi'i institutions in the United States, including the mosque in Toledo, Ohio. Funding such projects strongly suggests that the breach between the Shaykhis and the Usulis, once seen as insurmountable, has greatly diminished.[98]

Of course, the list of maraji' found at one mosque might not overlap with the list at another. For example, at the Irvine mosque apparently no one follows Khamene'i, while at another mosque in Detroit, the imam in charge mentioned Khamene'i in his short list of possible candidates. Obviously, their choices reflect the links that the ulama in the West have established with ulama back home, either through friendship, kinship, teacher/student relationships, or some combination of these factors.

There are, of course, subtle and not so subtle ways to influence the selection of the marja' in lieu of directly advising people. A large photograph in the mosque office of the Shaykh's marja' is certainly a strong indicator of his personal preference. However, once again, a Shaykh might feel that hanging such a photograph might be inappropriate and, possibly, seen as a divisive gesture. Certainly, when Khomeini and al-Khu'i were alive, a picture of either one in a mosque strongly implied the political leanings of that mosque, and invariably there would be people offended by such photographs. Today, a picture of Khamene'i as opposed to Sistani sends as clear a message of a political alliance or sympathy. Many mosques try to avoid the problem by attempting to ban any pictures of the maraji' in the mosques. But, as we will see, this is not always possible.

There are other means of using the mosque to influence the selection of a marja'. The itinerant preacher—a wa'iz or rawdakhwan—will have much more freedom in what he says than the regular shaykh of the mosque. He is invited to the mosque for a variety of possible reasons. He may be known as an eloquent speaker or for being very knowledgeable on a particular topic. He may be involved in some particular activity or have first-hand knowledge of certain events of interest to the congregation. He may also be brought in simply because he is in town and would be something of a novelty for the listeners. While it would not be to his benefit to alienate the congregation by saying anything that might offend the people, he also might be expected to express views that are not the usual fare. For example, one visiting 'alim expressed the view that, while it was important to follow a marja' and to pay khums, it was also important for the marja' to be responsive to the needs of the muqallid—giving emphasis to the latter part of the equation. Expressions of reverence and respect for the marja' are much more common during sermons. This 'alim was well aware of this fact, but he felt it was important for the

[98] JW: The Shaykhis are a sect within Twelver Shi'ism combining Akhbari literalism and a highly esoteric and philosophical theology. They are considered heretical by many Usuli Shi'a.

people to hear these views. He could risk being a bit unconventional because he was not going to have to face the congregation week after week and because they would have already known that he was a person with strong opinions and not beholden to any of the maraji‘. Also, he is sought after throughout the United States because of his well-known talent as a wa‘iz, being especially in demand during the months of Muharram, Ramadan, and Safar. To underscore both his sense of independence and his somewhat unconventional approach, it is interesting to note that he has on occasion asked me, an American woman and Christian, to address the mosque congregations during regular events. While this ‘alim did not make it his mission to express his choice on a particular marja‘, though he had his own short list of possibilities, others might be invited or given the opportunity to do just this. The head of the mosque can elect to distance himself from the speaker if he so chooses through subtle cues that everyone would understand but that would not be openly offensive to the speaker. The shaykh must avoid being a divisive element. Like a good politician, he must take into consideration his constituency, while still trying to adhere to his ideals.

When There Are Sunnis Involved

Occasionally there is another obstacle to openly promoting a marja‘, for sometimes there are Sunnis involved in the mosque. My own research in the Detroit area revealed that the segregation of Shi‘a and Sunnis in the mosques was quite complete. When the Shi‘i community became large enough to support its own mosque in the early 1960s, it set about building one, leaving behind the Sunnis with whom they had previously shared their religious lives.[99] However, this situation need not prevail in all local communities. If the Shi‘a have a mosque and the Sunnis in the area do not have one, or if the Sunni mosque simply is not convenient for prayer, Sunnis might opt to attend the Shi‘i mosque. Sunnis have no equivalent to a marja‘ and would find mention of the marja‘ during a mosque sermon to be very strange. The khatib or mosque leader needs to be aware of his audience and respond accordingly.

For example, at the Al-Khoei Foundation Mosque in Queens, New York, Sunnis attend the Jum‘a (Friday) prayers. The head of the mosque, Shaykh Sahlani, said that he was mindful of their presence and certainly knew that they would not be interested in a khutba that resonated with any exclusivist type of rhetoric. He also could not preach about the marja‘iya, a concept alien to the Sunnis. So, even at the mosque named in

[99] Linda Walbridge, *Without Forgetting*, pp. 44–47.

honor of a marja', there is sensitivity to teaching too openly about the institution of the marja'iya. On the other hand, in his office, hanging in a very prominent place, is a large, framed photograph of Ayatollah Sistani. A similar situation exists in the Al-Khoei Foundation schools in northwest London. These schools, one for boys and one for girls, operate as regular, full-time schools with a standard British curriculum to which religious instruction is added. The children who attend are from a relatively wide variety of sectarian and ethnic backgrounds, and, therefore, appropriately receive a more universalistic Muslim education. They do not learn directly about the marja'iya in their regular classes.

Strong public advocacy for one marja'—even among a group that appears to be quite homogenous—can backfire in Western mosques. As we have seen, politically active Shi'a—those who can be called "Islamists"—are not a monolithic group. There are a variety of factors that divide them, including issues of nationalism, specific ideologies, and personal allegiances. While Khomeini and al-Khu'i were still alive, an Islamic center opened in Dearborn that appealed to Shi'a who advocated a strict interpretation of Islam and who were generally supportive of the activist stance taken in Iran and Lebanon. However, even these opinions were not enough to bind together the group. One can, for example, admire Khomeini for some of his actions, while resenting him for others. Someone who was an ardent supporter of Baqir al-Sadr and understood his views would, more than likely, not wish to emulate Khomeini. Since the Shaykh of the mosque had studied in Qom, he was an ardent supporter of Khomeini both as a marja' and as a political figure and, consequently, alienated key people who might have supported his center. Contacts say that the center is now all but defunct.

Preference for the Non-Political Marja'

The marja'iya, as we have seen, can be a divisive issue. Yet, it has the potential to be a unifying force. Prior to the Iranian Revolution, there were Shi'a outside of the theological centers who either had not heard of the marja' or simply paid it little heed. While that situation has not completely changed, there is much more awareness of the marja', and people who wish to assert their Shi'i identity or become more devout in their practice of Shi'ism are likely to see the marja' as central to this personal transformation. This situation is not without its ironies, though. It appears that the person who gave the institution so much prestige, Ayatollah Khomeini, is also the person associated with the political radicalism and divisiveness that so many Shi'a reject.

It is obvious that Khomeini saw himself as the great liberating leader of the Shi'a of the world. While he carried on his revolution directly only in Iran, his rhetoric and attempts to export his radical ideology clearly show he meant to bring about a renaissance of Shi'ism through religio-political means. Key to the revolution was an institution that was already in place but, which, according to Khomeini, needed reinterpretation. This was the marja'iya. Khomeini reinterpreted it and seemed to infuse it with a great deal of potential power. He filled the role himself and, as a great charismatic figure, became a source of inspiration for a good many Shi'a. If nothing else, he made the believers feel proud of their religion because of his prestige throughout the world. He did the impossible: he led a revolution against a potentate who had the backing of the most powerful country in the world. Was this not a sign that the Day of Judgment was approaching?

There were serious problems with his endeavors to change Shi'ism, however. For one thing, he was out of touch with the modern world. Unlike Baqir al-Sadr, Khomeini did not attempt to understand the West and respond to it in a rational manner. He simply rejected it, yet the rank-and-file Shi'a cannot do that, especially those residing in the West. His legacy, then, is that of a medieval scholar who became a revolutionary, not of a scholar who could address the problems of living in the modern world in a rational way.

Of course, al-Khu'i up until 1992 and Sistani today are not concerned with "modernizing" Shi'ism per se, though Sistani is regarded as being "flexible," a theme we will come back to. It was that Khomeini was so adamant in condemning everything Western. That he drew such sharp boundaries between Shi'a and others in such a hostile, visible manner meant that to be Shi'a was to be unmistakably "the other." The fact that Khomeini's Iran was virtually at war with America placed Shi'a in a difficult position among their non-Muslim neighbors.

In addition, Khomeini went against a trend that had taken root among Shi'a, especially those who had come to the West escaping oppressive governments, war, and lack of opportunity. They wanted Shi'ism to be a religion and nothing else. Just as in the 1960s an American Catholic could begin to identify himself as a Roman Catholic without being seen as part of an anti-democratic, anti-American conspiracy, the Shi'a wanted to share in this experience also. While social integration in America may not have been a goal, professional and economic achievement was. To be discriminated against because of one's Shi'i identity became something to fear and avoid. Identifying with Khomeini and with Iran risked alienation from the greater society.

Al-Khu'i and Sistani, represent "purely religious" Shi'ism. One does not have to apologize for following either of them. Neither is not at odds with any Western government. Sistani was, in fact, essentially under guard by America's current enemy, Iraq. Not that mainstream Americans know about Sistani. Most have never heard of him or the marja'iya, yet the Shi'a can justifiably and honestly claim to be completely apolitical if they follow Sistani. They will not experience the cognitive dissonance felt by a person muqallid to Khomeini or to his ideological successor, 'Ali Khamene'i.

Those Who Do Not Follow Sistani

While more people are muqallid to Sistani than to any other grand ayatollah, the people who are muqallid to someone else need to be taken into consideration. Of course, some of these remain muqallid to al-Khu'i, as they have not experienced a need yet to make taqlid to a new marja', but these people are rapidly dwindling in number.

In the West, there are only two real competitors to Sistani for leadership: Khamene'i and Fadlallah. The other ayatollahs with aspirations for leadership and who are mentioned by Shi'a outside of Iran—Muntaziri, Ruhani, and Shirazi—do not have significant followings outside of the Middle East. Only Khamene'i is truly free to spread his reputation. Of course, in spreading his own reputation, he is principally attempting to boost the prestige of the Iranian government, which, in turn, promotes his marja'iya both in Iran and abroad. Khamene'i, principally a politician and not a scholar, cannot rely on some of the traditional means of building his marja'iya. As we have seen, al-Khu'i, as an example, had many students during his lifetime, and his students influenced others to become muqallid to him. As one informant said, "If a marja' has no students or very few, it is hard to develop a reputation."

We have seen that Sistani is prohibited from teaching because of the Iraqi government, yet he has still managed to build his reputation, mostly by having been recognized as the marja' by significant groups who, in turn, spread his marja'iya. But what about Khamene'i?

Khamene'i's association with the Iranian government works both for and against him. We have already mentioned the major disadvantages: the politicization of the marja'iya and the inability to attract students. The advantages, though, are significant. Khamene'i has not had to worry about raising money. He has the resources of the state behind him. Within Iran he is finding some success with the bazari class because of the favors he can perform for them as leader of the government. Outside Iran, he is also able to buy influence and set up organizations to counter those of other maraji'. The office that has been opened by Iran in London can be seen as a response to the Al-Khoei Foundation. However, it is mostly people who are already predisposed to following Khomeini's ideological successor who will follow Khamene'i. In some sense, he does not have to be concerned about spreading his reputation. In terms of the traditional marja'iya and the sorts of knowledge and qualities he is supposed to have, Khamene'i has no reputation to spread. He must rely on the fact that some Shi'a strongly wish to Islamicize government and society. This pertains to people living in the West, just as it does Shi'a residing in Iran and the rest of the Middle East. For these people, Khamene'i is the symbol of the victory of Islam over Western secularism. Alienated from Western values and traditions, they feel no discomfort with supporting someone who is so clearly at odds with the United States government. However, as noted earlier, these people constitute a minority. Thus far, the vast majority have voted with their pocketbooks for a non-political marja'.

Fadlallah, the Other Contender

During a visit to Leeds, England, I spoke with an Iranian who had been educated in a madrasa in Iran. He was involved in the mosque, formerly a church that had been remodeled to meet the needs of the Muslim community in that city. The mosque has a relatively extensive library available for sale, including works translated from Persian by William Chittick and Sachiko Murata. The mosque carried what this individual referred to as "the risalas" of 'Ali Khamene'i and Muhammad Fadlallah. Fadlallah's, he said, was greatly in demand by the mosque-goers.

In a mosque in Los Angeles I spoke to a woman in her 30s. Originally from Baghdad, she was working on a Ph.D. in one of the physical sciences. She had been drawn to the Islamist movement at least in part because of the influence of Baqir al-Sadr. Dressed in modified hijab, extremely articulate, especially about her ideas regarding women and their equality with men, she was muqallid to Fadlallah. She was well-versed in his opinions and believed that Fadlallah presented "the true Islam," an Islam highly compatible with the modern world. According to her, "Fadlallah, I think, is giving the correct view of Islam though we have never heard this before. Marriage, divorce, the form of the hijab, are all issues that he addresses. We don't have to wear traditional hijab, just things that meet the qualifications of modesty." In Detroit, a woman in her 40s from an old, highly prestigious ulama family—a person who wore conservative hijab—spoke glowingly of Fadlallah. Fadlallah, she said, was sensitive to the problems of the Shi'a who lived in the West, especially the youth.

Muhammad Fadlallah was on the United States terrorist list and excluded from entry into this country, yet his reputation and following continued to grow in the United States and Great Britain, especially among young Shi'ites. It was not his "involvement in terrorist activities" that explained his growing popularity. Rather, it is his progressive views on a wide variety of issues that earned him considerable respect. For example, one of the striking features found in the risalas of the maraji' is the focus on the *nijasa* of *kafirs*, the ritual impurity of non-believers, yet there is no actual textual basis for rulings that limit a Muslim's interactions with non-believers. The restrictions that are prescribed are based on what is referred to as "precaution," which is to say that it is better to ere on the side of caution by following rules that differentiate the ritually pure from the impure. Fadlallah disagrees with this argument. For him, everyone is tahir (pure) since there is no textual proof to decide otherwise. Such an opinion has far-reaching implications, especially for those who live among large numbers of non-Muslims.

Fadlallah's opinions also lead in the direction of permeable borders between Shi'a and other Muslims. Fadlallah has branded as having "no historical basis" stories that have been told for generations to express and perpetuate hostility towards Sunnis. The presence or lack of historical bases is very important for Fadlallah in formulating his opinions. He has faced severe rebuke for stating that the story of 'Umar and Abu Bakr pushing Fatima and causing her to miscarry lacks historical documentation. Again, for Shi'a living in the West where they might find good reasons to wish to bridge the gap with non-Shi'a Muslims, this sort of opinion is extremely liberating.

Fadlallah's "risala" is not in the usual format. It is actually a "questions and answers" book. One of its advantages is that it is accessible to the layman. Having books that are easily comprehensible, though, works against the specialist whose job it is to write and interpret this sort of work—i.e., the ulama. Part of Fadlallah's appeal to the youth is just this: he advocates handing their religion over to them and making the religious specialist less consequential in the practice of their religion.

As we have seen, there are different sorts of ulama. We can divide them into two broad camps: those who are legal specialists and those who are ritual specialists. Fadlallah, being a mujtahid, is a legal specialist. What is important to him are the laws that govern society and the individual's responsibilities in that society. The ritual specialist—be he called a rawdakhwan, a wa'iz, or a khatib—is not principally concerned with a rational approach to religion. He seeks to strike an emotional chord in his audience. It is his job to touch the hearts of the people and deepen their attachment to the central figures of the Faith. The legal specialist and the rawdakhwan are at the opposite ends of the religious continuum. They symbolize the head/heart dichotomy so commonly found in religions with well-developed theologies.

The traditional legal specialist or jurist—that is, most scholars who have gone through the madrasa education system—places the highest premium on the intricacies of the law and the philosophy behind that law. His job and his position in the religious hierarchy are considered paramount. He is revered for his learning, and, as we have seen, no attribute comes before being learned. While, to him, the work of the rawdakhwan is far inferior to his own, he tolerates it and sees its role in society. The rawdakhwan can be the rope that ties the people to their religion—the idea being that through their hearts their minds can be reached. Also, the rawdakhwan can act as an intermediary encouraging the people to follow a marja'. This is not to say that there is no competition between the rational legal scholar and the 'alim whose role it is to make people cry. In fact, Islamic societies are fraught with this struggle. It has become especially pronounced in the past few decades of this century as Islamic movements increasingly gain a foothold in the Islamic world.

Fadlallah's position—which grew out of that of the Iraqi opposition movement, al-Da'wa—differs from that of the traditional ulama. While to them the intricacies of the law are central to Shi'ism, Fadlallah prefers a simpler, less burdensome approach to legal and ritual matters. We saw that he wishes to do away with the concept of precaution, for example, signifying that he wishes to have a more straightforward approach to the texts. For Fadlallah, all opinions should have a textual basis. His followers in the West sound very much like the Sunni "fundamentalists" who place a high premium on using the Qur'an as the basis for their religious beliefs and practices. By placing so much emphasis on the Qur'an, of course, they are thereby diminishing the importance of centuries worth of opinions by the ulama.

Fadlallah's followers tend to be educated men and women who take their religion and religious education very seriously. They are not reluctant to challenge the opinion of an 'alim when they disagree, whether that 'alim be the shaykh of a local mosque or a marja' taqlid. For example, among certain Shi'a who have come to the United States, a point of contention for a number of years was the direction of the qibla. While al-Khu'i was alive, he said that the Shi'a in America should face southeast when they prayed. There were many engineers and scientists among these American Shi'a who firmly and clearly stated that the marja' was incorrect, that one should face northeast to pray.[100] Ayatollah al-Khu'i's

[100] JW: While a map might seem to indicate that Mecca is generally south-southeast of the United States, the shortest route to Mecca, the so-called great circle route followed by airplanes flying to Europe and the Middle East, goes northeast from the United States. In about 1990 I saw a globe in a mosque office in which a groove had been sawed in an attempt to support Ayatollah al-Khu'i's view. The imam involved was noncommital, saying that so long as one faced within ninety degrees of the qibla, one's prayer was valid. Ways of calculating

son, Muhammad-Taqi, in helping to design the Al-Khoei mosque in Queens, insisted that the niche in the mosque marking the direction of the qibla face southeast in keeping with the teachings of his illustrious father. The Shi'a who were aligned with the al-Da'wa movement and with Fadlallah's philosophy were adamant that this niche did not face the direction of the Qibla and, when they visited the mosque in Queens, they proceeded to pray facing northeast as others faced southeast! Their message was clear: the marja''s domain of expertise did not extend to scientific matters. Since his opinions went contrary to those of the scientists, it was to be ignored. For anyone who has listened to devout Shi'a speak about the marja' taqlid—whether they be traditionalists or sympathizers of Hezbollah—such opinions are startling. This latter group would be far more likely to claim that the marja' was infallible and that, if the marja' took an opinion on any issue, then that opinion would be considered true and legally binding.

Advocates of Fadlallah want explanations and sound, rational, scientific thought. They are not afraid to challenge the ulama, insisting that they don't want a local shaykh's opinion, but that of the marja' himself, often placing the layman and the ulama at odds with one another.

This is indeed an interesting development among the Shi'a. Michael Gilsenan, writing about ulama in Lebanon, pointed out the close relationship between shaykhs and young men.[101] It is these young men who most often surround the shaykh, attend his sermons, and participate in the rituals he leads. In Iran, the ulama were closely linked to young men and seen as their leaders—spiritually and militaristically. Yet, the "young people" who follow Fadlallah, many of whom are now responsible adults but still see themselves as a "new generation" of believers, are not so dependent on the ulama. Because they themselves are educated and feel quite capable of making their own judgments, they set a high standard for their ulama and do not tolerate haughtiness or condescension on their part. Just as they would judge a scientist, a physician, or an engineer by his abilities, so too they judge an 'alim by the keenness of his mind, the breadth of his knowledge, and his humility in listening to the opinions of others—even if they be laymen. As mentioned earlier, the founders of al-Da'wa had been affected by the Muslim Brotherhood, which is not ulama-based and has an anti-ulama element. Yet considering that al-Da'wa was founded by ulama and that it is so closely associated with Najaf, one

the direction of the qibla have, in fact, varied considerably over the centuries and in different Islamic countries.

101 Michael Gilsenan, *Recognizing Islam, an Anthropologist's Introduction* (London: Croom Helm, 1982), pp. 120–41.

of the great centers of Usuli Shi'ism, it is quite remarkable that the prestige of ulama did not rise in this group.

Such expressions of independence from the ulama place the al-Da'wa sympathizers at odds with other Shi'i activists, most notably Lebanese Hezbollah. Disagreeing with one's marja' is alien to Hezbollah. for whom the marja' defines the truth. The marja' is considered infallible and his infallibility has no limits. The gulf between Hezbollah and al-Da'wa is a serious one, in spite of the fact that both groups fall into the category of Islamic revivalists and are highly unpopular in the eyes of the United States government. When Shi'i activists hold meetings in the United States, they have to balance out their program with ulama and non-ulama speakers to appeal to a wide enough audience.

It is not only that the legal specialists' domain to be circumscribed, however. If the admirers of Fadlallah have their way, the role of the rawdakhwan will be diminished even more extensively. To those with an ultra-rationalist approach to Islam, mournful liturgical dramas hold no appeal. The rawdakhwan, of course, is trained to tell the story of the sufferings of the Imam Husayn and his family and followers in such a way that the listener could not helped being moved. Tears would be a natural reaction to listening to this tragic story. To Fadlallah's rationalist followers, the recounting of the story of Karbala should be a factual recounting of events and should avoid both the dramatic and the mythological element. It should be a somber, serious occasion, and not one where people wail and pound their heads and chests.

These attitudes and perspectives have the potential to make a major rift in the Shi'i community, yet this has not been the case. The congregation at a typical Shi'i mosque in the United States is a diverse group. The majority of Shi'a prefer an excellent rawdakhwan who stirs their spirits over a brilliant legal scholar familiar with all the intricacies found in scripture. While there is no consensus among Shi'a in the West, who are divided along ethnic, national, and ideological lines, on the issue of breast-beating and the dramatic expressions of remorse, it can be safely said that the ultra-rationalist Hizb al-Da'wa types have not succeeded in dominating the mosques, nor, for that matter, have the people who would wish for public displays of mourning with processions on the streets and public breast-beating. The Muharram commemorations are intense occasions, but they remain private affairs and ones where self-mutilation is not acceptable.

However, while the strongest force existing among the Shi'a community in the West is simply religious and cultural tradition, this does not mean that the forces for change have not had their effect, nor does it mean that the fight for separation of religion and politics has been won.

For example, a mosque referred to as the "Lebanese mosque" in Los Angeles was almost devoid of decoration during my visit there in March, 1996, except for a picture of 'Ali Khamene'i hanging alongside a picture of Khomeini, suggesting that those who frequent this mosque are aligned with Hezbollah, or are at least sympathetic to that cause. However, with further questioning it was found that the congregants at the mosque were more likely to be followers of Sistani than Khamene'i. Furthermore, there were also a substantial number of followers of Fadlallah who attended services at this mosque. Because of the diversity of opinion over the issue of the marja', it had been decided that no pictures would be hung. However, the Khamene'i supporters went ahead and hung Khamene'i's picture anyway. Once it was up, people felt reluctant to take it down. Such an act would have been considered unforgivably disrespectful to a marja'.

An interesting and potentially volatile situation arose when Shaykh Shams al-Din was visiting the United States in 1995. Shams al-Din, as the representative of Sistani, was visiting several Shi'i communities in the United States While in Dearborn, Michigan, he spoke out openly and vociferously against his rival, Fadlallah. As I reported, such openly divisive topics are not welcome in the Dearborn mosques as the majority of people there strive for at least some degree of harmony and consensus.[102] They certainly showed no indication of wanting Amal/Hezbollah clashes in their mosques, for example. Reports suggest that there was considerable anger at Shams al-Din for having been so critical of Fadlallah. Word of this event spread to Los Angeles, resulting in a refusal by the Lebanese mosque to invite him as a speaker when he was in California.

Tensions among the Believers

Open clashes have for the most part been avoided in Shi'i communities in the West. Having come from war-ravaged countries where religion has been such a divisive issue, the Shi'a are not eager for a recurrence of such rifts and violence. Yet, it is undeniable that tensions exist. Those interested in living by the letter of the law are critical of those who aren't, accusing them of compromising their principles and betraying the true nature of Islam. Those who are less legalistically-minded are suspicious of the "fanaticism" of the legalists, identifying them with "Khomeinism" and the politicization of religion. There are more subtle tensions, however, that would not be so obvious to the casual observer. These are among the believers who most definitely fall into the category of "Islamists" or Islamic revivalists but do not see eye to eye with others who also fall into

---

[102] Linda Walbridge, *Without Forgetting*, pp. 79–82, 119.

this category. The wearing of hijab or even of a cloak and turban does not automatically betray the religious ideology of any individual Shi'ite.

To show the subtleties of these tensions, it may be enlightening to look at Bint al-Huda, the sister of Baqir al-Sadr, and her legacy. While she never lived in the West, many of her admirers now do. She is a prototype of the new Shi'i woman and her reputation and approach to religion have not died. A university-educated woman from Baghdad now residing in London spoke excitedly about the effect Bint al-Huda had had on her and her mother. "Bint al-Huda was so loving, so understanding," she said. "You never felt like she was pressuring you to do anything." Another woman from a Najafi clerical family living in the United States was very interested in the prospect of having Bint al-Huda researched and written about in English so that people in the West could know about her. Pictures of Bint al-Huda show her in the all-encompassing abaya. To all appearances, she was the "invisible" Iraqi Shi'ite woman, yet she is famous for her advocacy of women's education and for their active involvement in the world. She is a model for women who wish to be true to their religion and its laws but who also want to be professional women.

Just as Bint al-Huda experienced criticism from her more traditional co-religionists, so too do her admirers in North American and England. In a less restrictive and traditional environment, these women will tend to wear modified hijab, rather than the abaya. Their clothing, while very modest, is practical for a work environment. A woman who has been influenced by Bint al-Huda is likely to be quite independent and assertive. She will likely select her own marja' and not rely on her menfolk to tell her whom to follow. (Bint al-Huda was actually muqallid to al-Khu'i, not to her brother, in spite of her obvious devotion to him.) Among these women, one is likely to find a good many who are muqallid to Fadlallah, whose opinions about women are the most progressive of all the leading ulama. These women, on the other hand, may very well be married to men who are muqallid to a more traditional marja'. This, as a matter of fact, is a problem that comes up repeatedly in meetings of Shi'a in the United States. The problem apparently is most striking and thorny on issues regarding concerns of ritual purity. For example, Fadlallah has interpreted the law to mean that the meat that comes from the ahl al-kitab—Christians and Jews—is halal and thus licit to eat. Khomeini, al-Khu'i, and Gulpaygani all said it was najis, impure, and that only meat ritually killed by Muslims was acceptable. Strict adherence to rules of ritual cleanliness for women has also been lessened. These would be particularly attractive rulings for women in Europe and North America who find themselves among non-Muslims and are less likely to be homebound. However, should a woman's husband or other family members not share her views, there is likely to be a conflict and one not easily rectified. The woman has the complete right according to religious law to be muqallid to whom she pleases. No one is at liberty to tell her to change her mind. A husband cannot go to the local shaykh and ask him to insist that she become muqallid to "the right" marja'. If the woman were actually breaking a law, if she were simply careless and negligent, it would be another thing. But this woman, by being able to cite her marja', is completely within her rights. However, this is not much consolation for the husband who is alarmed that all his ritual activities are being put into question by the actions of his "liberal" wife.

The segregation of women is another issue that plagues the Shi'a living in the West. Again, ethnic and national differences divide the community. Traditionally, Lebanese women have not been isolated from men in social occasions or in the home. The women from southern Iraq who have lived in the shadow of the shrines have not mingled with unrelated men. But it is not just tradition that prevails in the mosques and homes of Shi'a residing in the West. They have been influenced by a myriad of factors, including the teachings and interpretations of the maraji'. One woman who follows Fadlallah expressed annoyance that certain acquaintances of her husband object to her presence when they visit. In fairness, this situation also disturbed her husband, who disagrees with his friends' objections.

The Marja' as a Source of Unity and Discord

According to Shi'i law, taqlid is an obligation incumbent upon every believer. The conscientious Shi'ite is supposed to emulate a marja', the assumption being that one person will arise through consensus and be recognized as the leading jurist throughout the entire Shi'i world. While in the West there may be potential for the Shi'a to unify around one marja', this has not occurred yet. There is something paradoxical about the Shi'a/marja' relationship in the West. Since the death of Ayatollah al-Hakim, the majority of Shi'a who followed a marja', followed al-Khu'i. While he is described by some who were close to him as being "progressive," his views were very much in keeping with traditional religious rules and behaviors. He was no revolutionary. Then again, neither was he of special concern to the Shi'a. They might pay religious taxes to him. They might, now and then, consult his risala. However, they did not see him as being central to their religious life. Al-Khu'i, in a very limited manner, served as a unifying force because he reinforced the way Shi'a dealt with the world and did not make unpleasant demands on them.

After Khomeini became recognized as a marja' on a world scale, the issue of the marja'iya became far more vital and gained the potential to galvanize people. Khomeini had an urgent message and took a true leadership role. However, by having such a controversial message, he also caused great fission among the Shiʿa. Since Khomeini's death, the situation has only intensified, with divisions becoming more numerous and more subtle.

However, we still have been discussing the marjaʿ as though all Shiʿa actually did follow the law and made taqlid. This is hardly the case. In the next chapter we will look at those Shiʿa who have opted not to follow a marjaʿ at all, but still wish to be Shiʿa.

Chapter Nine

Those Who Are Not Muqallid

DR. FARID RECALLED that, when he was young, Ayatollah Shari'atmadari used to come to visit and study together with his father. One time, when he was seven or eight years of age, Ayatollah Shari'atmadari was visiting, and it was growing late. His mother would not serve dinner until she was sure that she would not have to feed the guests because she wanted to make sure there was plenty of food for them. The young Farid was very hungry, and he had been told that if he put salt in someone's shoes, they would leave. He kept taking pinches of salt and putting them in Shari'atmadari's shoes. When Shari'atmadari came to collect his shoes, he saw the salt in them and kindly said that he would not stay so late next time.

Dr. Farid's father was Ayatollah Sayyid Rida Musawi Zanjani. His grandfather was Sayyid Muhsin Musawi of Zanjan, who made a large fortune in nineteenth century Iran and left the next two generations of the family in independent circumstances. His mother's maternal grandfather was Sayyid Abu'l-Qasim Zanjani.

In Dr. Farid's pleasant, rural home west of Indianapolis, Indiana, is a framed plaque with a portrait of Prime Minister Mosaddeq in the center surrounded by pictures of members of his cabinet. At the top of the plaque is a picture of Dr. Farid's father, Ayatollah Zanjani, indicating that he was the spiritual guide of the Mosaddeq cabinet. Ayatollah Zanjani "followed" 'Abdu'l-Karim Ha'iri-Yazdi (referred to as "The Shaykh"), the person who founded the hawza in Qom. Dr. Farid, being born in 1925 and the son of an important 'alim, knew almost all the major Iranian clerics of the Revolutionary period. He recalls that his father, being wealthy, did not take any money for his religious services and that he could not be "bought" by the Shah. The Shah, he said, sent money for Zanjani "to pray for him," but Zanjani refused the money, saying that he always prayed for the Shah even without money. Farid says that this angered the Shah. Farid himself was arrested by SAVAK as the family was considered "too independent."

Dr. Farid made his hajj in the mid-1960s. At that time he had been muqallid to Ayatollah Milani, who also originated in Zanjan. He visited Milani in Mashhad after his pilgrimage. While never muqallid to al-Hakim, he thought favorably of him because he was "moving in a more liberal, open direction." For example, he said, al-Hakim said that meat served by Christians and Jews was halal. Al-Khu'i, he said, was too old to be a marja'. As of January 1996, Farid had never heard of Sistani.

Farid himself is not muqallid to anyone. His father, being a mujtahid, was not muqallid to anyone either, though he saw Ha'iri-Yazdi as a leader. Farid pays khums to a mulla in Iran and says that it is up to the mulla's conscience whom he gives the money to. He would find little in common with his fellow countrymen who are advocates of a theocracy. For him, religion and politics are two very separate matters. He broke off relations with the leader of the Dearborn Shi'i community, Shaykh Chirri, when Chirri began discussing Middle Eastern politics with the media. Chirri's comments could have been interpreted as expressing sympathy for hijackers and kidnappers, things with which Farid did not want his religion identified.

Farid is far more religiously oriented than his fellow Iranian expatriates of Shi'a backgrounds who now reside in central Indiana. His reputation for piety makes him popular among Iranians residing in the United States who are not religious but still want a person knowledgeable in religion to perform ceremonies for weddings and funerals. They do not have ulama, nor do they want them, so people such as Farid, who are not ulama but have a religious background are in demand for presiding at such occasions.

He has had forms printed up for marriage contracts. They are not legally binding by American standards but are considered "religious" contracts. Dr. Farid is one of several such individuals in the Iranian-American community who perform rites of passage among a population that, having once abandoned its religious traditions, is now seemingly trying to reinvent them. While the Arab Shi'a in the United States (and also in Great Britain) hire ulama to preach in their mosques and religious centers, to minister to their spiritual needs, and to perpetuate their ritual life, a substantial number of people of Iranian extraction who identify themselves as Muslims have gone in a very different direction.

This chapter is a brief exploration of what religious life is like among

Iranian Muslims in the United States who are seeking to maintain or to discover a spiritual direction in their lives. Ultimately, we hope to show how this community will effect the selection of the marja' and the role the institution might play in émigré communities.

Iranians in the United States

Refugees and immigrants to the United States are not uncommonly people who are unwanted by their home governments. When the Iranian Revolution occurred and the government fell under the control of clerics, the people who wished to leave Iran were the ones who were clearly not going to benefit from its government's policies and ideology.

Mehdi Bozorgmehr and Georges Sabagh[103] have written about the largest Iranian community in the United States, that of Los Angeles. Their data show that one-third of the immigrants and half of the exiles (people who came to escape persecution from the Iranian Republic) are either Jews or Baha'is. Jews also constitute a large proportion of the Iranians in the New York City area. The majority of Shi'a who came to the United States were from educated, middle-class backgrounds and did not want to live by Islamic law. From all outward appearances, it is impossible to differentiate one religious community from another. Except for a minority who are supporters of the Islamic Republic, the Iranians dress in modern, Western clothing and wear no conspicuous religious symbols, such as veils and beards. While among the Jews and Baha'is there is great variation in their degree of religious conviction and commitment, the Iranians of Shi'i background have tended to be emphatic that they are secularist and not religious.

I have spent a considerable amount of time among Iranians in the United States. I have found that, with relatively few exceptions, those from Shi'i backgrounds avoid discussion of religion even among—or perhaps especially among—other Iranians for fear that someone will think they are political. "Political" for them means being sympathetic to the ideas of Ayatollah Khomeini and the Iranian regime. They distance themselves as much as possible from the ideology of the Islamic Republic both in their criticism of the current regime and in their personal behavior and attire. They are also not likely to intersperse their speech with invocations of God's will. It is not uncommon to find them partaking of

---

103 Georges Sabagh and Mehdi Bozorgmehr, "Secular Immigrants: Religiosity and Ethnicity among Iranian Immigrants in Los Angeles," in Yvonne Yazbeck Haddad and Jane I. Smith, *Muslim Communities In North America* (Albany, N.Y.: State University of New York Press, 1994), pp. 445–73.

alcohol at social occasions. This is not to say that they have simply become "Americans," joined the great melting pot, and settled down to hot dogs, beer, and baseball. They actively strive to keep alive what they refer to as "Persian" (not Iranian) "culture." To say that Persian music, Persian cuisine, Persian crafts, Persian manners and etiquette, and Persian literature are still valued is a gross understatement. Persian concerts, movies, and celebrations of Persian holidays, particularly Nawruz, are anticipated and attended with great enthusiasm. Often their understanding of Shi'ism is superficial at best—especially for those who grew up in affluent Tehran away from the influence of the ulama and traditional, non-Westernized society.

Yet, when one scratches this very secular exterior, one can find some interesting surprises. Occasionally someone who appears totally alienated from the world of seminaries, mosques, and learned divines will wander off, with a little encouragement, into memories of early years in which religion had paid a central role in life. This is the case especially among those who had lived for a time in their youth outside of the middle-class areas of Tehran.

The Communist Atheist Who Was Muqallid to Isfahani

Dr. Shidnia, a highly respected and successful oncologist residing in Indianapolis, who now wears his white hair tied back in a ponytail, was a youth in Iran in the 1940s. Growing up in Isfahan, he was strongly influenced by his deeply religious mother, who was a sayyida, a female descendant of the Prophet. He had developed such a reputation for his religious devotion and sanctity that women would go to him when he was only twelve or thirteen and ask religious guidance from him. "In those days," he said, "I looked no one in the eye and always had my prayer beads in hand." However, in his later teens he began to question the credibility of the Twelfth Imam. "Then," he said, "I worked my way so far back through the Imams and the prophets and finally to God that I lost all religion." Going off to study in Tehran he turned to Communism and joined the Tudeh Party.

He apparently never looked back, giving the impression that religion is the least of his concerns. But a closer look reveals a more complex person. One evening at a party attended mostly by Iranians who had come to the United States in the pre-Revolutionary years, along with several descendents of Lebanese immigrants with an occasional northern European type sprinkled in the mix, I engaged Dr. Shidnia in a conversation about religion. His family had been muqallid to Ayatollah Abu'l-Qasim Isfahani. For a moment, though, he was unable to recall the Ayatollah's name. He closed his eyes and lightly beating his chest with his fist began quietly to chant some words. The chant jogged his memory as it had been used in praise of the grand Ayatollah. Isfahani resided in Najaf, but Dr. Shidnia recalls that when Isfahani visited Iran, Shidnia, who was by then a devout communist, went to hear him because he had once been muqallid to him and retained a residual sense of devotion to him. "After Isfahani's death," he said, "everyone then followed al-Hakim. It wasn't until after al-Hakim's death that all these other mujtahids claimed to be maraji'."

First, Dr. Shidnia's comment that "everyone followed al-Hakim" is indeed interesting, for he is Iranian, and it is supposed by everyone who writes about Iran that Borujirdi was the marja' that "everyone" followed. It appears that regional differences in Iran are stronger than is often supposed when it comes to religious matters, just as they are important in matters of culture. More important at the moment, though, is that Dr. Shidnia's former marja' could still stir some feelings of devotion in him. Even through the eyes of an atheist Communist, the grand ayatollah still appeared virtuous and worthy of respect. He never dismissed him as a charlatan or any other number of labels that are so frequently applied to men of the cloth by former believers. Once this veneer of irreligiosity was shattered, Dr. Shidnia revealed himself to have a good deal of residual attachment to his Shi'i traditions, including to the Imam Husayn.

Upon further questioning, I learned that Dr. Shidnia, like Dr. Farid, is also called upon to preside at weddings and funerals. His status in the community and his religious roots in Iran placed him in a different position from other Iranians in the area. While there are many others who are successful in their professions, they lack the religious education and reputation for devotion that Dr. Shidnia had those many years ago. His current lack of any open religiosity makes him an even more attractive candidate for his ceremonial role since those who request his services know that he will place no pressure on them to practice their religion.

A superficial look at the Iranian community in the United States would suggest that it is divided strictly down the middle between Khomeinists, who, as one Iraqi 'alim said, "will follow the party line and do whatever Khamene'i says," and those who completely reject religion because they associate it with the overthrow of the Shah and the establishment of the much-hated government of the Islamic Republic. Yet, as the cases of Drs. Farid and Shidnia suggest, this is definitely an oversimplification.

Children and the Need for Religion

A frequent subject among Iranians in social and educational gatherings is the fear that their children will lose their traditions, if they have not already done so. They express concerns for the erosion of parental authority and for the loss of the tradition of respect for elders and for proper manners. There is alarm that children have not or, if younger, will not, defer to the parents' wishes in choice of a spouse. Some express sorrow that the entire structure of Iranian values has simply been replaced by egocentrism and materialism. As Dr. Namaziqa, the head of the University of Southern California Dental School and the founder of the Iranian Muslim Association of North America put it,

> A majority of people who immigrated from Iran are Westernized people. However, they realized that for the first time in their lives, they are becoming a minority. There were a lot of places such as schools, mosques, hospitals, etc., for them in Iran, but not here. They realized that they are getting older and that they need to join a group or organization to fill the empty spaces in their daily lives. Separation from culture, separation of their children from the culture and religion created a big generation gap and value conflicts.

Other immigrants and exiles from Islamic countries, of course, express the same misgivings about life in America. Their response is either to send their children to the mosques for religious training or at least to talk about doing so. The secular Iranians do not have this recourse. They do not have mosques. During a visit to Westwood, California, I struck up a conversation with a waiter in a Persian restaurant and inquired as to whether there were any mosques that the Iranians in the area attended. "Yes," he replied. "There is small one in a cemetery very close by." Directions in hand, I found the cemetery and, in pouring rain, found an office at its far end. The people in the office were at first confused by the reference to a mosque on the cemetery grounds, but then realized that the man in the restaurant was referring to the small chapel next door where Iranians gather for memorial services. In one of the largest Iranian communities in the United States, there are no mosques and no ulama.

Of course, there are mosques in the greater Los Angeles area. However, the majority of Iranians in the area are anti-Islamic Republic and would not attend a mosque frequented by pro-Republic Iranians. Nor would they be likely to attend the other mosques in the area, which are led and frequented by Iraqis, Lebanese, and Pakistanis, and where sexual segregation and veiling are practiced.

For the most part, parents have been left on their own to find ways to educate their children in the values and virtues they hold dear, with varying degrees of success. The loneliness of this endeavor, along with a sense of spiritual emptiness that often accompanies life in America for many immigrants and exiles, has forced some of the members of the Iranian community to take action to help alleviate their problems. As one prominent member of the community in the Los Angeles area said, "People are going back to their religious roots. They have religious gatherings which are fashionable among Iranians now." This trend took a while in coming, partly because of the negative image given by the media, but also because of a lack of trust and a lack of experience in institution building among the community members themselves.

The Nature of Religion Among the Iranians

Those affiliated with IMAN have been meeting in a YMCA located in Southhill. Hasan Shahbaz, editor of a Persian-language journal, referred to this group as "religious Iranians but not ones who side with the Islamic Republic." Like other Shi‘a, they come together for Ramadan and birthdays of the Ahl al-Bayt and to commemorate Muharram. However, there is no lamentation during Muharram. The commemoration consists of "talk about the history of Karbala and about the life of the Imam Husayn, his personality, and what he has done. They have singers who sing poems about Imam Husayn. The Iranians are particularly attached to the Imam ‘Ali and, even if they do not fast on any other occasion, will be likely to fast on his date of death." No ulama speak or lead prayers at these meetings. This role is filled by people such Dr. Namaziqa, who has held prayers every Thursday night in his home since the late 1980s. He said that the celebration of Laylat al-Qadar, the night that the Qur'an was revealed, drew nine hundred people for a program that lasted from 8:30 p.m. to 2:30 a.m. In the near future it is expected that such events will be held at a large Islamic center in West Los Angeles, which is being funded by wealthy members of the local community.

Mr. Shahbaz, when invited to speak at these religious gatherings, talks about "divine love" and quotes from the great Persian poets, Rumi and Hafez. He is concerned with topics such as mysticism and gnosticism and about how people can reach God through their own belief. Dr. Namaziqa reiterated this notion of private belief. "We are not trying to direct people to a particular approach to religion. We are not under the influence of any scholar (mujtahid). People are free to follow any doctrine and practice in any form they want." He predicts that "they can ultimately come to a conclusion of how they want to see their religion expressed by combining all ideas to come to a solution supported by a majority of leaders." The basis of the religion is, according to Dr. Namaziqa, "to obey the Qur'an and the *Nahj al-Bulagha* (a collection of the sermons of the Imam ‘Ali), and to follow the Prophet's Sunna and the Ahl al-Bayt leadership." It most emphatically is not to follow a marja‘ taqlid.

Mr. Kamiabi-pour is another activist now living in the Los Angeles area who, as he has grown older, has felt a strong need to help lead the Iranian community back to religion. Mr. Shahbaz's daughter, Guity, referred to him in an earlier interview as a person who had grown religious and whose wife now wore a headscarf. A former diplomat with the Iranian foreign ministry, he commented, "Before modern times it was necessary to make taqlid. If you did not, you were not a Shi'i. But today books are available for everyone to read." It is interesting to note that Mr. Kamiabi-pour praised 'Allama Tabataba'i[104] for "having adapted the traditional way so that everyone can understand it." 'Allama Tabataba'i, according to Dabashi, was severely rebuked by Ayatollah Borujirdi for teaching philosophy, specifically the works of Mulla Sadra, when he first arrived in Qom. Borujirdi was emphatic that only traditional courses should be taught. Dabashi reports that, while Tabataba'i presented his defense for teaching philosophy to young people who were being affected by other ideologies, particularly communism, he ultimately stated his obedience to his marja' taqlid, Borujirdi. Borujirdi, after this, ceased in his criticism of Tabataba'i, and the 'Allama continued to teach Mulla Sadra. It is 'Allama Tabataba'i's interest in the works of Mulla Sadra that Mr. Kamiabi-pour found particularly attractive.[105]

It would be tempting to say that the Iranians in the United States are moving towards Sufism (Islamic mysticism), which has acted as an alternative to ulama-based religion in many parts of the world. There is a strong strand of Sufism in Iran, one that the ulama felt obligated to suppress. Indeed, there are Sufi groups in the Los Angeles area, but the people who are gravitating to IMAN and similar organizations are not members of a Sufi group. Dr. Namaziqa, considers these Sufi groups to be about as fanatical as are the supporters of the Islamic Republic. While he rejects Sufism, he does see a place in religion for 'irfan (mystical knowledge), which, he says, can be applied to any religious tradition, again leading to the idea that there is common ground for religious unity.

Mr. Kamyabi-pour, whose organization, The International Council for the Promotion of Science and Culture of the Qur'an, is a rival of IMAN, differs somewhat in his approach. "I like Sufism and 'irfan," he said, "but they do not come before the Shari'a. First, there is the Shari'a,

---

104 JW: Muḥammad-Ḥusayn Ṭabāṭabā'ī (1904–81) was a prominent philosopher in Qom well known for his encyclopedic commentary on the Qur'an, *al-Mizan,* in twenty volumes. He was a teacher of a number of ulama prominent in the Islamic revolution. On his life and thought see Dabashi, *Theology,* pp. 273–323.

105 JW: Mullā Ṣadrā (d. 1640) was the greatest Iranian and Islamic philosopher of the early modern period. His works combine Neoplatonism and mysticism. He is, more or less, the official philosopher of the Islamic Republic of Iran. Ayatollah Khamane'i's brother runs an institute devoted to studying and propagating his philosophy.

then tariqa (the path to God), and then truth. Without Shari'a you can't get to the next stages."

Yet, exactly how Shari'a is interpreted is not the same for all believers. While anyone who is muqallid to a marja' would consider it almost unthinkable not to fast during Ramadan, regardless of the environment in which he or she is living, Mr. Kamyabi-pour's opinion is that fasting is very difficult here in the West, and "it can paralyze you from normal life. So, if you find it difficult to do your job when fasting, you do not have to fast." An Iraqi who is muqallid to al-Khu'i but follows Fadlallah for new issues said that during Ramadan all the Muslims in his office in the Los Angeles area fasted except for the Iranians. The Iranians to whom he referred might well understand Mr. Kamyabi-pour's sentiments on religion and fasting, but they were quite alien to this Iraqi Shi'ite.

American Iranians and the Marja'iya

The Iranians in the United States who are "rediscovering" their religious roots present an interesting contrast with many of their coreligionists in the West. Bitterly resenting the takeover of their government by "religious fanatics," they avoid contact with Iranians in the West who remain loyal to the Islamic Republic. This anger (and fear) of political Iranian Shi'a have made them suspicious of any group of Muslims who adhere closely to Islamic law and exhibit outward signs of religiosity. At this point in their history, the main preoccupation of most Iranians residing in the United States is to maintain their cultural identity. If they are to develop religious institutions, it will be within the framework of Iranian cultural traditions. There is no real interest expressed in bridging cultural gaps between themselves and other ethnic and national communities.

The move towards a more religious atmosphere among many of these Iranians is a new phenomenon and no firm conclusions can be made as to what direction it will go. There is apparently considerable disagreement among the active members of the community as to what is acceptable and what is not. These disagreements have been reflected in the organizations that have been founded to promote Islam.

Still, one can detect certain common themes, the most important being that the Shi'i ulama are not welcome in the lives of the people or in their religious centers. While there are men to lead prayers and to read scripture and even to give enlightening sermons at Islamic centers, there are no ulama to keep alive the traditions and laws that so clearly differentiate the Shi'a from everyone else. The resistance to having ulama in religious centers is hardly surprising. If these Iranians were not active supporters of the Shah, they were at least supporters of secular values.

The religious lives of clerics from Qom would be nearly as alien to them as would be the lives of Buddhist monks.

Unlike Dr. Farid in central Indiana, who grew up in a clerical household, most of these people will not be paying khums. Money designated for religious purposes, therefore, will go directly to the community. This also means that no marja‘ is going to be involved with the building of mosques or religious schools, which in turn means that the reputation of the ulama and the marja‘ taqlid will not be promoted in the community. The marja‘ needs the muqallid for his survival. If the muqallids ignore the marja‘, it is as if the marja‘ ceases to exist.

Of course there are Iranians in the United States and Europe who do follow a marja‘, generally Khamene'i, but they are in a minority. They also keep a low profile so as not to attract attention from monarchists, leftists, and, not least, the American government. This situation weakens the impact that the Iranian marja‘iya, and by default the Iranian government, have abroad.

As the Muslim community grows in size and importance in the West, religious institutions are going to be increasingly reliant on members of this community. Just as American Catholics are a force that the Pope has had to deal with, so will the major centers of Islamic learning have to acknowledge American Muslims. While other Shi‘a residing in the United States, particularly Arabic-speaking communities, Khojas, and others, such as Pakistanis, have built strong bonds with the ulama in Najaf, the majority of the Iranians in the United States have turned away from the ulama, placing Qom at a relative disadvantage.

Iranians and Other Muslims

Whether this group wants to be differentiated from others is debatable. An elderly Iranian ‘alim who now resides in the Los Angeles area said that he had been devoted to bridging the gap between Sunnis and Shi‘a but had met with resistance from other Shi‘a. Dr. Farid also supports an ecumenical approach to religion and expressed his opinion that the division between Sunnis and Shi‘a is inappropriate in the modern world. These views tend to be shared by Shi‘a who are not concerned with the intricacies of Islamic law, who do not look to the ulama for guidance, and who have never suffered religious persecution for their Shi‘ism. It may be assumed that a rational view of the situation will lead to an ecumenical approach and to the uniting of various sects and factions of the Islamic community. However, religion is not always based on rational concerns. There are ties that can bind people to a tradition that have little to do with rational, theological arguments.

To many Iranians religion and cultural artifacts and events merge into a coherent whole. Nawruz, for example, is originally a Zoroastrian, not a Muslim holiday, yet Khomeini found it impossible to prevent its celebration in Iran, regardless of people's religious orientation. This holiday has been usurped by Iranian Shi'a as part of their own tradition. While Nawruz is not celebrated exclusively by Iranians, it is not a holiday shared by Arabs, Khojas, Pakistanis, or other major Shi'i groups. Nor do the vast numbers of Sunnis in the world celebrate Nawruz. None of these groups would approve of holding such celebrations in their centers and mosques. Other aspects of Persian culture—food, poetry, and music—that are so highly valued by Iranians are also stumbling bonds to unifying the Iranians with other Shi'a or other Muslims. Most Iranians residing outside of Iran do not desire an austere, "fundamentalist" approach to religion. An austere Islam of prayers and fasting is not what they seek. Religion, unadorned with the beauty of their culture, is simply no religion at all.

Oddly enough, though, some of the comments made by these Iranian religious leaders, suggest that, through different avenues, they have actually come to some of the same conclusions as other non-Iranian Shi'i activists about whom I have written. Challenging the ulama, asserting one's own ability to read and comprehend scripture, and finding innovative ways to address modern issues are ideas that have been presented earlier. Followers of Fadlallah, for example, are inclined to think that they have every right to question man-made laws, regardless of how high the lawmaker is in the eyes of the community. The followers of Fadlallah and the Iranians currently under discussion would not be likely to acknowledge any similarities. The Iranians are likely to dismiss anyone who is muqallid to a marja' as being a fanatic. The Iranians, in turn, would be judged as non-religious regardless of their protestations to the contrary.

The fact that there are diverse groups of Shi'a looking for ways to adapt to the modern world while retaining or re-establishing their religious identity suggests that in the long run, there may be a way to build a larger, more broadly-based religious community. At this point, ethnicity and nationality play a large role in determining the nature of the religious life of any given community. However, if the Shi'a are at all similar to other religious groups who immigrated to the United States, nationality will slowly become less consequential. Catholic churches that were once "German" or "Polish" are now simply Catholic churches.

If Shi'ism is revived among the majority of Iranians in this country, future generations, less entrenched in cultural traditions, may seek a way to bridge gaps with other groups, including other groups of Shi'a. They may all be eager to find a way to express their religious devotion but still be very much part of a modern, scientific world.

If Shi'ism is revived among the majority of Iranians in this country, future generations, less entrenched in cultural traditions, may seek a way to bridge gaps with other groups, including other groups of Shi'a. They may all be eager to find a way to express their religious devotion but still be very much part of a modern, scientific world.

Glossary

Adhan: The call to prayer

Ahl al-Bayt: The family of the Prophet Muhammad, in particular the Prophet, his daughter Fatima, their sons Hasan and Husayn, and the remaining nine Imams

Ahl al-Kitāb: Non-Muslim monotheists, particularly Jews and Christians

Akhbār: Reported sayings of the Prophet and the twelve Imams

Akhbārī: A Shi'ite legal school stressing the text of the sayings of the Prophet and the Imams and discouraging inference.

A'lam: "Most learned," a qualification of the marja' taqlid

'Ālim, pl. 'ulamā': "The learned," Islamic clerics

Ayatollah (Āyat Allāh): "Sign of God," title used for maraji' and distinguished mujtahids

Baḥth al-khārij : "The external level," advanced seminars in Islamic law

Banū Hāshim: The Prophet's clan and their descendants

Bāzārī: Traditional bazaar merchant

Bid'a: Innovation, discouraged in Islamic law

Dār al-Islām: The Islamic lands

al-Da'wa, Ḥizb al-Da'wa: An Iraqi Shi'ite political party

Faqīh: Islamic legal scholar

Fiqh: Islamic law

Ḥadīth: A reported saying of the Prophet

Ḥalāl: Legally permitted

Ḥarām: Legally prohibited

Ḥawza: A complex of Shi'ite educational institutions in a particular city, usually Najaf, Karbala, or Qom

Hezbollah (Ḥizb Allāh): "The Party of God," a Qur'anic term referring to the Islamic community and taken as the name of political parties in Iraq and Lebanon

Ḥusaynīya: A hall for reciting the sufferings of the Imams

'Ibādāt: Ritual rules in Islamic law

Ijāza: A license to teach a body or body of knowledge or to represent a particular marja'

Ijtihād: Independent inference in Islamic law

Imām: In Shi'ism one of the rightful successors of the Prophet; also the prayer leader in a mosque

Imām jum'a: The preacher who leads Friday noon prayers at the main mosque of a city

'Irfān: A Shi'ite form of mysticism

Ismā'īlīs: A branch of Shi'ism recognizing a different line of Imams

Ithnā-'Asharī: Twelver, the term for the main Shi'ite group, which recognize twelve legitimate successors of the Prophet

Kāfir: A non-believer

Khaṭīb: A preacher

Khojas: A Shi'ite group originating from India that was originally Isma'ili but part of which became Twelver Shi'ites

Khums: "The fifth," a religious tax of a fifth of an individuals net income after living expenses

Khuṭba: mosque sermon

Madrasa: A religious school

Marja' taqlīd, pl. marāji' taqlīd: "Source of emulation," the highest rank of Shi'ite cleric

Marja'iya: The institution of the marja' taqlid

Mu'āmalāt: Transactions, a branch of Islamic law

Muḥtāṭ: "Out of caution, precaution," an action taken because it might be religiously required

Mujtahid: A Shi'ite legal scholar with the expertise to make independent judgments about Islamic law

Muqallid: Someone who follows the judgments of a particular marja'

Nā'ib: The representative of a marja'

Najis, nijāsa: Impure, impurity

Nawruz: The Iranian new year, approximately March 20

Occultation (ghayba): The period in which the Twelfth Imam is absent

Qibla: The direction faced in during Muslim prayers

Rawḍa: The recitation of the sufferings of the Imams, particularly Husayn

Rawḍakhwān: The Persian term for a preacher specializing in reciting the sufferings of the Imams

Risāla: "Treatise," often referring to a manual of Islamic law written by a marja' taqlid for the use of his followers

Sahm al-Imām: Half of the khums reserved for the Hidden Imam

Sahm al-sādāt: Half of the khums reserved for needy descendants of the Prophet

Sayyid, pl. Sādāt: A male descendenat of the Prophet

Sayyida: A female descendenat of the Prophet

Shaykh: Title of an Islamic scholar, usually not a sayyid

Shaykhī: A Shi'ite sect founded in the eighteenth century with a strongly philosophical bent

Sufism: Islamic mysticism

Sunnī: The main Islamic sect recognizing the elected caliphs as the Prophet's legitimate successors

Tablīgh: Islamic proseletizing

Ṭāhir: Ritually pure

Ṭālib, pl. Ṭalaba: A theology student

Taqīya: dissembling one's faith to avoid danger

Taqlīd: Following the authority of a marja' taqlid

Traditions (ḥadīth): The reported sayings of the Prophet

Umma: The Islamic community

Uṣūl al-fiqh: The principles of jurisprudence, the rules by which Islamic law is deduced

Uṣūlī: A Shi'ite legal school that accepts the legitimacy of ijtihad

Wā'iẓ: A preacher

Wakīl: The representative of a marja' taqlis

Walī faqīh: The supreme marja' who thus has supreme political authority according to Khomeini's theory

Wāsṭa (properly wāsiṭa): Mediation, connections

Wilāyat al-faqīh: The theory, promulgated by Khomeini, that the supreme marja' ought to exercise supreme political power

Wuḍū': Ritual ablutions

Zakāt: religious tax common to Sunnīs and Shī'a

Bibliography

Abrahamian, Ervand. *Khomeinism.* (Berkeley, CA, 1993).

Akhavi, Shahrough. "State Formation and Consolidating in Twentieth-Century Iran: The Reza Shah Period and the Islamic Republic." In Ali Banuazizi,and Myron Weiner. *The State, Religion, and Ethnic Politics: Afghanistan, Iran, and Pakistan.* [Syracuse, N.Y.]: Syracuse University Press, 1986.

Amanat, Abbas. *Resurrection and Renewal: The Making of the Babi Movement in Iran,* 1844–1850. Ithaca, NY: Cornell University Press, 1989.

Arjomand, Said Amir. *The Shadow of God and the Hidden Imam: Religion, Political Order, and Societal Change in Shi'ite Iran from the Beginning to 1890.* Publications of the Center for Middle Eastern Studies 17. Chicago: University of Chicago Press, 1984.

Ashraf, Ahmad. "Bazaar-Mosque Alliance: The Social Basis of Revolts and Revolutions." *Politics, Culture, and Society* 1 (1988). Pp. 538–67.

———. "Theocracy and Charisma: New Men of Power in Iran." *International Journal of Politics, Culture, and Society* 4/1 (1990). Pp. 113-152.

Aziz, Talib M. "Baqir al-Sadr's Quest for the Marja'iya. In Linda S. Walbridge, ed., *The Most Learned of the Shi'ah.* Pp. 140–48.

———. "The Islamic Political Theory of Muhammad Baqir al-Sadr." Dissertation, University of Utah, 1991.

———. "The Role of Muhammad Baqir al-Sadr in Shi'i Political Activism in Iraq from 1958 to 1980." *International Journal of Middle East Studies* 25/2 (1993), pp. 207-222.

Baram, Amatzia. "The Radical Shi'ite Opposition Movements in Iraq," In Emanuel Sivan and Menachem Friedman, eds. *Religious Radicalism and Politics in the Middle East.* Albany, NY: State University of New York Press, 1990. Pp. 95-125.

Batatu, Hanna, *The Old Social Classes and the Revolutionary Movements of Iraq: A Study of Iraq's Old Landed and Commercial Classes and of Its Communists, Ba'thists, and Free Officers.* Princeton: Princeton University Press, 1978.

———. "Shi'i Organizations in Iraq: al-Da'wah al-Islamiyah and al-Mujahidin." In Juan R. I. Cole and Nikki R. Keddie, eds. *Shi'ism and Social Protest.* Pp. 179-200.

Chamberlain, Michael. *Knowledge and Social Practice In Medieval Damascus, 1190-1350.* Cambridge: Cambridge University Press, 1994.

Cole, Juan R. I. "Imami Jurisprudence and the Role of the Ulama: Mortaza Ansari on Emulating the Supreme Exemplar." In Nikki R. Keddie, ed. *Religion and Politics in Iran.* Pp. 33-46.

———. ""Indian Money' and the Shi'i Shrine Cities of Iraq, 1786–1850." *Middle Eastern Studies* 22/4 (1986), pp. 461–80.

———. "Mafia, Mob and Shiism in Iraq: The Rebellion of Ottoman Karbala." *Past and Present* 112 (1986). Pp. 112–143.

———. *Sacred Space and Holy War: The Politics, Culture and History of Shi'ite Islam.* London: I. B. Tauris, 2002.

———, and Nikki R. Keddie, eds. *Shi'ism and Social Protest.* New Haven, CT: Yale University Press, 1986.

Cottam, Richard. "Nationalism in the Middle East: A Behavioural Approach." In Said Amir Arjomand, ed. *From Nationalism to Revolutionary Islam.* Albany, NY: State University of New York Press, State University of New York Press, 1984. Pp. 28-52.

Cunningham, Robert, and Yasin K Sarayrah. *Wasta: The Hidden Force In Middle Eastern Society.* Westport, Conn.: Praeger, 1993.

Dabashi, Hamid. *Theology of Discontent: The Ideological Foundation of the Islamic Revolution in Iran.* New York: New York University Press, 1993.

Daftary, Farhad. *The Ismā'īlīs: Their History and Doctrines.* 2nd ed. Cambridge: Cambridge University Press, 2007.

Faḍl Allāh, Muḥammad-Ḥusayn. *Khaṭawāt 'Alā Ṭarīq al-Islam.* Beirut: Dār al-Ta'āruf, 1985.

———. *Min Waḥy al-Qur'ān.* 3rd ed. Beirut: Dār al-Zahrā', 1985.

———. *Qaḍāyānā 'alā Ḍaw' al-Islām.* 1973.

———. *Ta'ammulāt Islāmīya ḥawla al-Mar'ah.* [Beirut] : Dār al-Malāk, 1992.

——— and Salīm al-Hasanī. *al-Ma'ālim al-Jadīda li'l-Marja'īya al-Shī'īya.* Beirut: Dār al-Malāk, 1993.

Fischer, Michael M. J. *Iran: From Religious Dispute to Revolution.* Harvard Studies in Cultural Anthrolopogy 3. Cambridge: Harvard University Press, 1980.

Gellner, Ernest. "Tribalism and the State in the Middle East." In Philip S. Khoury and Joseph Kostiner. *Tribes and State Formation In the Middle East.* Pp. 109–26.

Gilsenan, Michael. *Recognizing Islam, an Anthropologist's Introduction.* London: Croom Helm, 1982.

Haddad, Yvonne Yazbeck, and Jane I Smith. *Muslim Communities In North America.* Albany, N.Y.: State University of New York Press, 1994.

al-Hairi, Kazim. *Tarjamat Ḥayāt al-Marja' al-Ṣadr.* Qum, Iran: 1988.

Haskins, Charles Homer. *The Rise of Universities.* Cornell: Cornell University press, 1957.

Hunter, Shireen. *The Politics of Islamic Revivalism: Diversity and Unity.* Bloomington: Indiana University Press, 1988.

Jamali, Fadil. "The Theological Colleges of Najaf," *Muslim World* 50 (1960), pp. 15–22.

Kazemi Moussavi, Ahmad. "The Institutionalization of Marja'-i Taqlid in the Nineteenth Century Shi'ite Community." *The Muslim World* 84/3-4 (1994), pp 279-299.

Keddie, Nikki R., ed. *Religion and Politics in Iran: Shi'ism from Quietism to Revolution.* New Haven, CT: Yale University Press, 1983.

Kedourie, Elie. "The Iraqi Shi'is and Their Fate." In Martin Kramer, ed. *Shi'ism: Resistance and Revolution.* Boulder, CO: Westview, 1987. Pp. 135-157.

Khomeini, Ruhullah. *A Clarification of Questions.* Trans. J. Borujerdi. Boulder: Westview, 1984.

Khoury, Philip S., and Joseph Kostiner. *Tribes and State Formation In the Middle East.* Berkeley: University of California Press, 1990.

Khūrī, Fu'ād Isḥāq. *Imams and Emirs: State, Religion and Sects In Islam.* London: Saqi, 1990.

———. *Tribe and State in Bahrain: The Transformation of Social and Political Authority in an Arab State.* Publications of the Center for Middle Eastern Studies 14. Chicago: University of Chicago Press, 1980.

Kostiner, Joseph. "Kuwait and Bahrain." In Shireen Hunter. *The Politics of Islamic Revivalism.* Pp. 116–29.

Lambton, Ann. "A Reconsideration of the Postion of the Marja' al-Taqlid and the Religious Institution." *Studia Islamica* 20 (1964). Pp. 115–35.

Lapidus, Ira M. "Tribes and State Formation in the Middle East." In Philip S. Khoury and Joseph Kostiner. *Tribes and State Formation In the Middle East.* Pp. 25–47.

Mallat, Chibli. "Iraq." In Shireen Hunter. *The Politics of Islamic Revivalism.* Pp. 71–87.

———. *The Renewal of Islamic Law: Muhammad Baqer As-Sadr, Najaf, and the Shi'i International.* Cambridge: Cambridge University Press, 1993.

Marr, Phebe. *The Modern History of Iraq.* Boulder, Colo.: Westview, 1985.

Momen, Moojan. *An Introduction to Shi'i Islam.* Oxford: George Ronald, 1985.

Mottahedeh, Roy. "The Islamic Movement: The Case for Democratic Inclusion." *Contention* 4/3 (1995), pp. 107-27.

Nakash, Yitzhak. "The Conversion of Iraq's Tribes to Shi'ism." *International Journal of Middle East Studies* 26/3 (1994), pp. 443-463.

———. *The Shi'is of Iraq.* Princeton, NJ: Princeton University Press, 1994.

Norton, Augustus Richard. "Shi'ism and Social Protest in Lebanon." In Juan R. I. Cole and Nikki R. Keddie. *Shi'ism and Social Protest.* Pp. 156-178.

Rose, Gregory. "Velayat-e Faqih and the Recovery of Islamic Identity in the Thought of Ayatollah Khomeini." In Nikki R. Keddie, ed. *Religion and Politics in Iran.* New Haven, CT: Yale University Press, 1983. Pp. 166-188.

Ramazani, R. K. "Shi'ism in the Persian Gulf." In Juan R. I. Cole and Nikki R. Keddie, eds. *Shi'ism and Social Protest.* Pp. 30-54.

Sabagh, Georges, and Mehdi Bozorgmehr. "Secular Immigrants: Religiosity and Ethnicity among Iranian Immigrants in Los Angeles." In Haddad and Smith. *Muslim Communities in North America.* Pp. 445–73.

Sachedina, Abdulaziz Abdulhussein. *The Just Ruler* (al-Sultān al-'Ādil) *in Shī'ite Islam: The Comprehensive Authority of the Jurist In Imamite Jurisprudence.* New York: Oxford University Press, 1988.

Sarūr, 'A. Ḥ. *Faḍl Allāh wa-Taḥaddī al-Mamnū'.* [Lebanon]: Tawzī' al-Sharika al-'Āmmah li'l-Khadamāt al-Inmā'īya, 1992.

Trix, Frances, John Walbridge, and Linda S. Walbridge, eds. *Muslim Voices in the Modern World.* New York: Palgrave Macmillan, 2008.

Walbridge, Linda S., ed. *The Most Learned of the Shi'a: The Institution of the* Marja' Taqlīd. New York: Oxford, 2001.

Walbridge, John and Linda. "Master Singer of Pakistan: Baba Shafqat." In Trix et al, eds. *Muslim Voices in the Modern World.* Pp. 43–55.

———. "Son of an Ayatollah: Majid al-Khu'i." In Trix et al, eds. *Muslim Voices in the Modern World.* Pp. 101–11.

Walbridge, Linda. *Without Forgetting the Imam: Lebanese Shi'ism in an American Community* Detroit: Wayne State University Press, 1997.

———, ed. *The Most Learned of the Shi'a: The Institution of the* Marja' Taqlid. New York: Oxford University Press, 2001.

Wiley, Joyce *The Islamic Movement of Iraqi Shi'as.* Boulder, Colo.: Lynne Rienner Publishers, 1992.

Woodward, Bob, *Veil: The Secret Wars of the CIA, 1981-1987.* New York: Simon and Schuster, 1987.

Index

ABOUT THE AUTHOR

LINDA STRICKLAND WALBRIDGE
was born19 October 1946 in Camden, New Jersey. She was an anthropologist specializing in minorities in the Islamic world. She received a B.S. in psychology from Southern Connecticut State College in 1971 and an M.S. in psychology from the American University of Beirut in 1973. She worked for a number of years as a psychologist before returning for a doctorate in anthropology at Wayne State University, which she received in 1991. She was the assistant director of the Middle East Institute at Columbia University from 1991 to 1993. She published her dissertation as *Without Forgetting the Imam* in 1996, received a Fulbright Fellowship to Indonesia in 1997, and spent eighteen months in Pakistan between 1998 and 2001, where she did the research for her book,
The Christians of Pakistan: The Passion of Bishop John Joseph (2002).
She also edited a volume on Shi'ite religious leadership
(*The Most Learned of the Shi'ah: The Institution of the Marja' Taqlid,* 2001).
She died 9 December 2002 in Bloomington, Indiana.
She was beginning to resume work on the present book
at the time of her death.

JOHN WALBRIDGE
is Professor of Near Eastern Languages and Cultures
at Indiana University, Bloomington.

26355122R00106

Made in the USA
Charleston, SC
04 February 2014